AUTHORS TAKE SIDES ON THE FALKLANDS

THE QUESTIONS

Are you for, or against, our Government's response to the Argentine annexation of the Falkland Islands?

How, in your view, should the dispute in the South Atlantic be resolved?

AUTHORS
TAKE
SIDES
ON
THE FALKLANDS

Two Questions on the Falklands conflict answered by more than a hundred mainly British authors

Edited by

CECIL WOOLF and JEAN MOORCROFT WILSON

CECIL WOOLF PUBLISHERS, LONDON

First published 1982
©1982 Cecil Woolf Publishers

Cecil Woolf Publishers, 1 Mornington Place, London NW17RP
Tel: 01-387 2394

ISBN 0-900821-63-9 hardback edition
ISBN 0-900821-62-0 paperback edition

Contents

Stop Press!

Introduction

Contributions from the following authors arrived too late for inclusion in the main body of the book and appear on pages 109 to 121:

Paul Ableman
Dannie Abse
Kingsley Amis
Thomas Balogh
Melvyn Bragg
Raymond Briggs
André Brink
Arthur Hailey
Elizabeth Jennings
Colin MacCabe
Derwent May
Ivor Montagu
Jan Morris
Robert Nye
Roland Penrose
Tom Pickard
John Rae
George Wigg

Introduction

Stop Press!

Contributions from the following authors arrived too late
for inclusion in the main body of the book and appear on
pages 119 to 121:

Nine weeks after the Argentine invasion of the Falkland
Islands, following the breakdown of several diplomatic
initiatives, Mrs Thatcher ordered the task force to retake
the islands. Between then and the surrender of the Argentine
garrison at Port Stanley, we sent out two questions to about
a hundred and fifty authors in Britain, America and a few
other English-speaking countries (the questionnaire is
printed in full on page 135).

>   Are you for, or against, our Government's response to
> the Argentine annexation of the Falkland Islands?
>   How, in your view, should the dispute in the South
> Atlantic be resolved?

The reader who opens this book may ask himself why
we chose to canvas and record the views of writers on the
brief conflict in the South Atlantic. What, it may be said,
do writers know of such matters? This is a political issue;
why don't you turn to the politicians? One of the answers
is that we chose writers because in most cases they were
not politicians and might therefore be felt to stand outside
the immediate fray. It is surely not irrelevant to have the
opinions of a cross-section of the intellectual community.
Another powerful argument for canvassing writers is that
they tend to be people of imagination, a quality which
seemed to us mostly lacking in the political response to the
crisis. This, of course, applies to all creative artists, but
writers could be expected to be the most articulate.

Those approached were writers in the broadest sense,
novelists, poets, playwrights, journalists, humorists, as well
as writers on specialised subjects, such as history, philosophy,
science and politics. The responses were equally varied,

coming as they did, not only from full-time writers but also from from less predictable sources. They included university professors, an anglican clergyman, a doctor, a magistrate, an astronomer, some comedians, an ex-lorry-driver, one member of the House of Commons and four members of the Lords. One journalist had actually interviewed General Galtieri during the conflict.

To begin with we noticed that a number of writers seemed unwilling to reply, in contrast with the flood of answers received initially to *Authors Take Sides on Vietnam*. We began to suspect that this hesitation was related to the fact the Government has throughout implied that anyone who criticised them was, to use the Prime Minister's phrase, 'stabbing our boys in the back'. Several authors refer to this attempt to stifle debate, which was also evident in the Government's criticism of the media, particularly the *Panorama* programme in which minority views were expressed. It was largely to counteract this tendency that we determined to produce a book which could provide a much-needed forum for discussion.

One of the earliest contributors, in a letter accompanying her piece, emphasised another way in which the debate had been distorted:

> I am grateful to you for giving writers this opportunity of making our views on the Falklands known, against the clamour of the popular press and media programmes, who seem to have found in this idiotic situation an end-less and exciting fund of popular entertainment for a public so habituated to simulated violence that they hardly discriminate between fiction and the real thing.

It could be argued that since over a hundred out of about 150 authors responded that authors felt uninhibited by the popular newspapers' and Government's attempts to mute criticism. However, a closer look at the answers suggests that this is in fact not the case. All the replies are dated, either by the authors in the course of their pieces or by the editors from the letters. It is significant that, while the

fighting was in progress, fewer pieces were received than
after it was over. It was also noticeable that as time went
on more contributors tended to oppose the Government
than support it, presumably because they had had time to
consider the consequences.

It ought to be emphasised that the authors were chosen
regardless of any known opinions, since our object was to
obtain a random mix. At the beginning one of us was for
the Government's response and one against, so we had no
real problems about being fair in our choice: if we had,
inevitably, prejudices they had to be equally balanced. In
the few cases where writers who were also politicians were
canvassed, we did consciously weigh our selection. Tam
Dalyell, for instance, was invited together with Enoch
Powell, Edward Heath with Michael Foot, while in the
Lords George Wigg and Thomas Balogh were
counterbalanced by Max Beloff and John Julius Norwich.
After we had made what we hoped was a fair list we
wrote to the writers and then left it entirely to them. No
pressure was put on people to reply and no attempt was
made to influence the outcome. In addition, all replies
responding to the questions have been published. Finally,
there has been no editing of the pieces, unless specifically
requested by the authors on, for instance, grammatical
grounds. In this we were guided by Salvador de
Madariaga's advice, that 'men of letters should have the
freedom to bring you their flowers with stems, roots and
even some earth attached to them'. One of our main
concerns throughout has been to achieve as great a degree
of objectivity as possible.

It was also in the cause of objectivity that we finally
decided on an alphabetical arrangement of the pieces. In
Nancy Cunard's *Authors Take Sides on the Spanish War*
writers were divided into For, Against and Neutral. For
Authors Take Sides on Vietnam a more sophisticated
ordering was devised. In both cases the arrangement was
open to criticism of editorial tinkering. Since, as already
stated, we wished to be as objective as possible, we opted

for the balder but less biased order of the alphabet.

Turning to the pieces themselves, what struck us from the beginning was the low proportion of those who were neutral, less than ten per cent. It was also noticeable that, at the outset, opinion was almost equally divided between those for and against the Government's response. As time went on, however, those opposed to the Government increased until, in the final poll of 106, approximately 39 were for, 59 against and eight appeared to be neutral.

However, very few pieces are as straightforward as the above breakdown suggests and the ultimate picture is far from black and white. To some extent the pieces reflect the varying attitudes adopted by members of Parliament. The hard-line war party is represented, though its members are few. Then there are those who support the Government's dispatch of the task force and their use of it to retake the islands, but who would like to see Mrs Thatcher ready to negotiate. Next come those who back the sending of the task force but *not* the use of it. Finally there are those who oppose the whole exercise from start to finish, arguing that it was not worth the spilling of one drop of blood. It is interesting to note that a number of writers who were opposed to American intervention in Vietnam support the British Government in the Falklands.

Attitudes towards the United Nations also vary widely. Some contributors are dismissive of it, while others firmly believe that the dispute provided an opportunity for the UN to develop as an effective institution for maintaining world peace.

Some writers argue that national credibility and pride were at stake in the Falklands' conflict, it was a 'national humiliation *not* to be borne'. It also posed, they claim, a major threat to the security of other small nations and provinces, such as Gibralter, the Channel Islands and even the Isle of Wight! Some see it, ultimately, as a threat to our very survival. Aggression, they assert, must not be seen to pay.

Another argument put forward is our duty to the

islanders: we could not abandon them to the not so tender mercies of a fascist regime. On the other side there are those who argue that we could safely do precisely that, pointing to the sizeable Welsh and Scots communities in Argentina, or compensate each islander so handsomely that they could choose where they wished to live.

At least one writer, whilst praising the 'heroic courage shown in all our services', feels that a bitter lesson has been learnt, namely 'that we should have a large and totally modern navy'.

A number of writers compare the Argentine junta with the leaders of nazi Germany and conclude that, just as we had no choice but to fight Hitler, so we had to oppose Galtieri. Equally there are those who argue that it was not a situation comparable with the Second World War: to use one writer's words, 'it was *not* a war of national survival' and therefore not justifiable.

One of the strongest arguments in favour of the Government's action is that it was a matter of 'principle'. We could not allow a large country to walk in and take over a small one. In answer to this various cases are cited to show that this Government was not preoccupied with 'principle' when the people concerned were black, as are the Diego Garcians. Nor were previous governments ready to help Greek Cypriots against 'fascist' Turkey. East Timor provides yet another example.

A number of writers refer to the historical and legal aspect of the conflict. Surprisingly few of them question the legality of Britain's claim to sovereignty, though both *The Sunday Times* and *The Times* carried articles on the secret doubts of the Foreign Office concerning our legal title over a long period of time.

One frequent theme to emerge from these pieces is the necessity for pacifism, particularly in a nuclear age. Holders of this view are not confined to those who oppose the Government's action. Paradoxically several supporters of military action to retake the islands also subscribe to the notion that settling disputes by war is an anachronism.

Another pervasive theme is what one author calls 'bonapartism' in both governments. That is, the device by which leaders deflect criticism of their domestic policies by pointing to glories abroad. Even more sinister motives were perceived by some for the Government's response, such as the testing of new weapons, both for 'defence' purposes and as a shop-window for our arms industry, and a test of the preparedness of the nation.

Yet another consideration that arises is not merely the cost of the campaign and the future garrison, but also the expense involved in the Government's implicit commitment to develop the islands. This seems to some writers shameful in view of the drastic cuts imposed by the Government in education, health and other social services for financial reasons.

Some authors express anxiety about future co-operation and understanding between the English-speaking world and Latin America. It is clear, they say, that the Government have from the beginning failed to understand the Latin American temperament with its lofty notion of pride.

Another set of writers see the war as the last throw of a former world-power clinging desperately to its remnants of empire.

The nearest the contributors come to unanimity is in their condemnation of the junta and, almost equally, in their reservations about our own Government's handling of the situation. Even their staunchest defenders tend to criticise them for allowing the crisis to develop in the first place. They are also criticised for their willingness to sell arms to the Argentines up to the last moment, even though they condemned their regime with extreme self-righteousness during the war. One writer particularly objects to what he calls Mrs Thatcher's 'demeanour', which was he claims 'bellicose'. Others assert that the sinking of the *General Belgrano* 35 miles outside the exclusion zone was a deliberate act of provocation which made further negotiations with the Argentinians fruitless. Many people suggest that an appeal to the International Court, together

with sanctions and a blockade, should have been tried
before sending the task force and that the Government
were too anxious to engage in hostilities. As one writer argues,
this would have had the advantage of giving us time to
marshal the necessary air-cover, which, as others intimate,
the task force lacked.

Solutions to the problem range from retaining the islands
with a strong garrison for as long as necessary, to negotiating
a settlement either as soon as possible or after feelings
have been allowed to calm down. Several people would like
to see the UN called in to arbitrate and a few suggest
partition as the most sensible answer. Everyone seems
nervous of the probable cost to Britain.

In a survey of authors such as this it seems appropriate
to find people appealing to literary authorities. A number
invoke Shakespeare, calling on different texts. Many quote
Dr Johnson's dictum that 'patriotism is the last refuge of
a scoundrel'. One writer finds Henry Miller's 'mentally
[man] is on all fours' appropriate, whilst another believes
E.F. Schumacher's 'small is beautiful'. At least two authors
call on the Bible, both Old and New Testament, to support
their arguments. Southey, Schiller, Brecht and Proudhon
are all allowed their say. Gandhi is quoted as replying, when
asked what he thought of Western civilisation, 'I think it
would be a very good idea'.

Wit was also very much in evidence. One author defines
a Falkland island as 'a small piece of land entirely surrounded by advice'. Another refers to the Falklands' 'imported
and exploited slave-class of—sheep'. Yet a third sees the
conflict as 'a war to save Mrs Thatcher's face, which may,
in time, become as notorious as Jenkins's ear'. The
reservation follows: 'It is not a face worth launching a
thousand ships, or even a task force, to rescue.'

When we sent out the questionnaire on which this book
is based, politicians were predicting a protracted struggle.
In the event, the battle for the Falkland Islands lasted barely
three weeks. It was an extraordinarily difficult issue and
one which divided friends, families, political parties and

the country at large. A month after the fall of the Argentine garrison the debate continues and the reader will, we hope, share our interest and enthusiasm. Future historians may also find in this book a valuable record of intelligent contemporary opinions on the Falklands' conflict.

CECIL WOOLF & JEAN MOORCROFT WILSON

the country at large. A month after the battle for the
garrison the debate continues and the reader will, we hope,
share our interest and enthusiasm. Future historians may
also find in this book a valuable record of intelligent
contemporary opinion on the Falklands conflict.

CECIL WOOLF & JEAN MOORCROFT WILSON

THE ANSWERS

Joan Aiken

If this is an example of democratic action (and we must
fear that it is, since opinion polls have shown a majority
of both Argentine and British populations in favour of
military action) then it seems conclusive proof that
democracy is not a practical means of government. Any
rational adjudicator would have offered the Falkland islanders a sufficient sum to establish themselves elsewhere in the
world and a government pension thereafter; this would have
saved millions of pounds. Economic sanctions should have
been applied to Argentina much more severely as punishment for aggression; what has happened since is the
inevitable result of trying to counter violence with violence.
8 June 1982

Brian Aldiss

If you leave the back door open day and night, it is useless
complaining when thieves walk in and steal your silver.
Lord Shackleton's survey of the Falklands was neglected
by successive governments; governmental and public
indifference to the islands — characterised by Dr Johnson
as places where 'a garrison must be kept in a state that
contemplates with envy the exiles of Siberia' — was total.
Small wonder the Argentinians felt that it was no great
crime to walk in, small wonder they called the first belligerent British response 'over-reaction'. So it must have
seemed. The blame at that stage was ours, and more
particularly, I suppose, the Foreign Office's.

Whatever follows from such an unsatisfactory beginning

15

must be unsatisfactory. The least distasteful outcome is
for us, the British, now to complete the course upon
which we have recklessly embarked: that is, to win the
islands back, since success is always to be preferred to
defeat. But while the majority of the country clamours
for blood, and the tabloids run headlines like 'Up Your
Junta!', high-principled talk about preservation of sacred
democratic ideals is hypocrisy.

One good thing may emerge from the present embarras-
ments; the supporters of unilateral disarmament may
become less vociferous.

As to how the dispute should be resolved, for preference
I would like to see the islands sink below the waves which
cast them up.
11 June 1982

John Arden

I write on the day (15.6.82) when it seems that the fighting
is over, though whether this means an end to the war in
toto is not yet clear. This has been one of the silliest and
most scandalously unnecessary wars in the history of
British arms. It has produced a situation in which all the
problems that were there to be negotiated before the fighting broke out are still there, to be negotiated, though in a
far less amenable political climate. Small military 'aggressions'
can always be 'defeated' if large enough forces are ranged
against them, and if prime ministers are sufficiently resolute
at the expense of other peoples' lives. As the Anglo-Irish
absentee landlord so courageously said in the 19th century:
'If the tenants think that by shooting my bailiff they can
intimidate *me*, they are sorely mistaken.' The whole thing
has in fact been an attempt (successful? surely not?) to
replenish some of the international reputation lost by
Britain during the failure, last year, to criminalise the
political prisoners in the northern Irish gaols. That exercise

in Mrs Thatcher's Caligula-like 'immovable rigour' caused
the deaths of ten hunger strikers: this time she has lost
rather more young men, not all of them Argentinians. It all
contributes, I daresay, to an amelioration of the unemployment crisis, as also will the work of replacing those
singularly inflammable warships. Her government is not to
be congratulated upon concealing its original incompetence
by a temporarily successful batch of manslaughters. I am
only glad to have been living in a country (Ireland) where
there was a government which took a humane and judicious
view of the sorry situation. My mail from Britain has
shown me that not everyone there has been infected by
the emotional barbarism of most of the London press. I
hope the next general election will not take place before
the real nature of these gladiatorial orgies has become
clear to the voting public. Territorial disputes are to be
sorted out in the UN: this one could have been so dealt
with if London had taken it seriously enough soon enough.

A.J. Ayer

Briefly, I am opposed to the action which the Government
has taken over the Falkland Islands. I think it probable that
we shall regain possession of the territory, but I do not
think that this is a long-term solution to the problem and
even if it were I do not think that it would justify the loss
of life, on both sides, the enormous expense, the emergence
of the ugly face of jingoism and the alienation of even the
more democratic countries in Central and South America.
29 May 1982

C.J. Bartlett

It is possible that the British government by skilful use of
the carrot and stick before April 1982 might have averted

the present crisis. Even a *modus vivendi* now seems much
more elusive. Domestic political considerations have been
allowed to exert too much influence on foreign policy in
both countries. Attractive as it might be, it is not possible
to treat this crisis simply as a worthy struggle against an
irresponsible and harsh regime. But if neither reasoned
dialogue nor force offers an obvious way forward, one
must expect the future of the Falklands to be determined
by as yet unforeseeable internal and external pressures on
the two governments, especially once other issues begin to
demand greater attention and resources. It will be surprising
if the South Atlantic question is resolved on its merits or
in the light of reason.
7 June 1982

Max Beloff

As an active and committed supporter of the present
Government, my answers would be:
1. I am for the Government's response to Argentine aggression — 'annexation' is the wrong word since the Argentines
claim the islands have always been theirs, and most of the
rest of the world denies that legitimate possession can
derive from aggression.
2. I do not see how the dispute can be resolved until an
Argentine government accepts defeat and is prepared for
genuine negotiation on what role it might have in the
Falklands. That will take a long time. Meanwhile we must
defend the islands and islanders as best we may.
10 June 1982

Michael Bogdanov

A choice between an exocet and a hospital, a sea-king and
a school. What sane person would not opt for welfare before
war?
22 June 1982

Vincent Brome

When we first discovered the Falklands in 1592 international law — so far as it existed — said 'he who discovers owns'. In the early nineteenth century when we took over the Falklands international law had changed. It was socially acceptable to annexe territory by force. Today international law-and-or morality has refined these crudities out of existence and any country invading another's territory by force breaks international law. That is the historic perspective. Geographically Argentina has a claim to the Falklands, but then so has France to the Channel Islands.

The key question remains. Was it worth amassing a mightly armada to challenge a totalitarian regime which had flagrantly violated international law. Philosophically the question was a perennial old chestnut. If by sacrificing a few hundred people you help to preserve the fabric on which Western civilisation depends are you justified? There is no black and white answer.

The United Nations? It is not an organisation which can enforce its rulings as exemplified by 502. We have twice gone to the International Court only to be told by the Argentinians that if the issue is pre-empted in their favour they will abide by its decisions! Pre-emption is of the essence of their position.

What remains? A tragedy. Appalling loss of life and mutilation in the interests of a small community of 1,800 people who could have been absorbed in Britain. None the less, with the utmost reluctance, I have to agree that upstart dictators who have no regard for human rights in their own country cannot be allowed to get away with flaunting international law and imposing their brutal values on people who reject them. It is tragic that we should be the self-elected instrument for doing what the United Nations cannot do. But once we have achieved that end the United Nations should reappear and take over.
1 June 1982

Brigid Brophy

Mrs Thatcher is a rarity among prime ministers in that she went to war for the purpose of defeating her own policy. For two years her government sought to disembarrass Britain of responsibility for the Falkland archipelago. It then mounted a military campaign to recover the territory it had been trying to get rid of. That paradoxical action was the only honourable course it had left open to itself to pursue when the Argentines incontinently invaded the islands the British government wanted to give them. In this collision of governmental ineptitudes people were killed.

By a further paradox, this history has been interpreted in Britain as evidence of Mrs Thatcher's undeviating firmness of will. In reality, it was a spectacular U-turn. Mrs Thatcher was outwitted and outwilled by 1,800 unsophisticated Falkland Islanders. The war was between two sides who were really on the same side but had failed to make it clear to one another, with the result that it was the wishes of the Falkland Islanders that prevailed in defiance of them both. Mrs Thatcher will probably turn out to have committed Britain not only to garrisoning but to 're-developing' the Falkland Islands, thereby contradicting the policy she resolutely applies to the British Islands, which is to leave them un-re-developed and in the condition of a post-industrial slum.

Mrs Thatcher's political self-defeat has been called a victory. It is difficult not to conclude that the British Islanders are so childish and so dangerous that they prefer the excitement of bloodshed to good government. If there was a victory of the Falklands it was won in 1977 by the Labour government of James Callaghan, which deterred an Argentine invasion without destroying a life. There is a cause in which a task force should sail to the Falkland archipelago, namely to protect its indigenous population of whales, fish and birds, together with its imported and exploited slave-class of sheep, from murder.
24 June 1982

Alan Brownjohn

The answer to the first question is, Against. The belief that
international wrongs may be permanently righted by force
of arms is—in the nuclear age above all—monstrous,
irresponsible lunacy.

This is the day after the surrender at Port Stanley, 15th
June. The relief is enormous; but there is not the faintest
reason to hope that the Falklands problem is solved. Mrs
Thatcher has just talked in the House of Commons about
'the dominance of Britain'. What poverty of historical and
human imagination! Nothing is more certain to guarantee
that the Argentine, under Galtieri or an even more odious
replacement, will go on demanding 'the dominance of
Argentina' and working to achieve it.

We have had, in the Falklands, what someone correctly
called 'an infra-nuclear war'. It has been far less appalling
in its brief course than Vietnam, but conceivably more
sinister in its implications. War has moved on since the
1960s, and the dealers in electronic military aids are eating
very well. Computer-programmed death has been profitably
and impersonally dealt at large distances near the Falklands
in the last two months. On BBC-1 Mr John Nott denied
that it was like *Star Wars*. But the South Atlantic has most
certainly been a testing ground for the refinement of the
newest deadly weapons—and the blood and screaming has
been kept as comfortably remote to most of Britain and
Argentina as a video game.

Now the only 'lessons' consistently talked about are the
military ones: how to make the weapons even deadlier
next time. The end of this War is, in fact, a terrible, frightening moment. War has, for Britain, been made permissible
and sufferable once more. Genuine lessons for humanity
about the overwhelming importance of the United Nations
have been torn up. What *could* be done now—the answer
to the second question—is to secure at least the chance of
a long-term peaceful solution by committing the Falklands
to the trusteeship of the United Nations, soliciting the aid

of the United States and Latin America. But Thatcher currently rejects the United Nations option with contempt.

There is more we can learn from the Falklands experience. Some of these other lessons are intensely shocking; some are even more intensely alarming.

We have still to come to terms with the poison left in the system by the imperial legacy. Britain can still apparently produce governments and leaders whose murderous self-righteousness can take the breath away. Such governments can still depend on vicious and ignorant newspapers, which now switch from soft-core pornography to hard-hat chauvinism with no difficulty. They can trust in broadcasters to play along with ministerial euphemism and misinformation (who has ever clearly told us that the General Belgrano was *two hundred nautical miles* from the task force when it was sunk with the loss of 368 lives?) They can rely on clerics who will wear their moral atrophy with pride.

The machinery of darkness is in good trim. It can apparently be started up very quickly to distract attention from a Prime Minister's domestic embarrassments. We *are* a better nation than Thatcher makes us seem. But we will find our post-imperial adulthood in the international community only when we have dismantled the evil engines of the past.

There is another, much worse, truth to come to terms with. We have lived with the Bomb for so long that the language of warning is almost exhausted, whether it comes in hyperbole or understatement. So one can only repeat it as coolly and levelly as possible: The Falklands War has made it indisputably obvious that a British Government would kill as many of us as it liked (perhaps all of us) if it thought the cause was right. In the South Atlantic Thatcher was playing a game called Better Dead than Not British.

Another time the stakes could be higher. We can all easily imagine the Ministry of Defence spokesman, in his bunker, drily enunciating details of nuclear strikes and acceptable megacasualties. As the likelihood of nuclear conflict inexorably increases, so the 'defence' provided by nuclear weapons looks more and more of a deception — and the faith of our Governments in nuclear deterrence strengthens. In no nuclear war could Britain survive. The Falklands War, an electronic rehearsal marketed with obsolete rhetoric, brings such a war closer by implying that it could be fought with 'professionalism', and 'honour', and at little cost.

I do not think there has been in my lifetime a moment of so little hope.

Peter Cadogan

Since it is easy to be wise after the event I shall quote what I wrote on 6th April: 'A shocking disaster threatens. Regaining the Falkland Islands is Mrs Thatcher's express objective and there is now no doubt that the Argentines will fight. Are we to connive in the deaths of thousands of Britons and Argentines in a war to defend a ghastly mistake made by Mrs Thatcher, the Foreign Office and the Ministry of Defence? Surely not!' Memorandum: Falkland Islands Emergency.

The casualties were less than I expected, partly because a high proportion of the direct hits suffered by the Task Force were by dud bombs; but at the same time there is no way of quantifying what the Task Force put up with during long weeks at sea and both sides in nights spent in the open in wet freezing peat bogs. The sinkings were serious and had they included the *Hermes, Invincible* and *QE2* would have been decisive. Both sides were wrong. The Argentines in Madrid issued a statement reported in *The Financial Times* on 18th May condemning both the original invasion and Mrs Thatcher's military response, and that, I take it, is the correct attitude.

There was another response that was never tried. Argentina was, and is, bankrupt. Debts in March amounted to 32 billion dollars with 7 billion to find this year. Those debts have since risen to 45 and 11 billions respectively. (*Sunday Times*, 20th June). The rate of inflation was 180% and that has increased to 200%. Argentina is on its knees. London and Washington had Galtieri over a barrel and they let him go because financial sanctions (that stopped the Suez operation in four days in 1956) would have had repercussions at home. Blood was cheaper.

We took the islands by force in 1833, lost and regained them by force in 1982. There is no moral issue, it is all a question of battalions. The Argentine claim to the islands is impeccable on pre-1833 grounds and the British case is equally impeccable (on grounds of prescription) over the years since 1833. What we have failed to understand is that the Falklands/Malvinas issue is a *religious* matter in Argentina. That the Malvinas are Argentina's is part of the *credo* by which the Argentines identify themselves; and people will live and die for a sacred object despite its patent non-rationality. We discount this at our peril. The issue was also a God-given subject for bonapartism for both Galtieri and Mrs Thatcher: glory abroad as antidote for sickness at home.

The Falklands are a fag-end of empire. The Foreign Office has long known this and tried its best to off-load the problem, but the ethos of empire survives the eclipse of empire and eighteen MPs of all parties hammered Nicholas Ridley when he brought the matter to the attention of the Commons as recently as 1980. The Falkland Islands Council was similarly determined to live in the past. The islanders have their full share of blame.

Ideally the best answer is a UN Trusteeship but that will only be possible if all parties agree. It would be worth trying. If it is not possible then some other formula has to be worked out with the Argentines. Mrs Thatcher has made a shocking mistake in ruling out both the UN and negotiations with Argentina and that, in my view, will be her undoing. The fortress-Falklands idea is absurd. There are 100,000 people of British descent living well in Argentina and there is no objection in principle to adding a mere 1,800 to their number. The military nightmare will pass. There have been six military regimes at various times since 1930 and none of them have lasted. The return to civil government is already on the cards.

The alarming thing has been the political mirror held up to the UK by the whole experience. We discovered the meaning and scale of British tribalism. Some 80% unthinkingly followed the flag, 14% presented a totally ineffective opposition—and that gives good cause for a lot of thinking.

21 June 1982

James Cameron

Of course I am against the current British operation in the Falkland Islands.

I have expressed that opposition in print so often now that anything I say is bound to be a repetition.

I oppose a multi-million pound exercise by an allegedly bankrupt country to retain a few Atlantic islands that have no meaning for us, never had any meaning for us, of which hardly any of us had heard until the other day. And whose inhabitants, incidentally, have so far no legal right to claim citizens' residence in the UK.

Of course I cannot condone the unwelcome intrusion of an atrocious regime like that of the Argentinas. I think I would feel exactly the same if the Argentinians decided to annexe the Channel Islands, which seems to me almost analogous.

I cannot think of a more suitable case to formally test and try out the formal authority of the United Nations.

At the same time I cannot but feel and hope that by the time your book could be published the unpleasant and preposterous situation will have been resolved, though God knows how.

27 May 1982

Jilly Cooper

All I can say is I think Mrs Thatcher was magnificent, our troops even better.

I'm desperately sorry for the families of all those who died on both sides. But I have to confess some of those Argentinian officers are so frightfully goodlooking one might almost enjoy being taken prisoner by them.

Ian Macdonald for president!
22 June 1982

Roald Dahl

In 1939 we were all prepared to risk our skins to fight against aggression. Today, excessive socialism seems to have nurtured a flabby and idle breed of people who would rather compromise than fight. I would fight. Thank goodness there are some left who would do the same.
7th June 1982

Tam Dalyell

Since the Government's response was dictated by considerations of injured political pride, and the future careers of leading politicians, rather than concern for the islanders, I am contemptuous of it (and no less contemptuous of the ill-thought-out gut reaction of some of my own friends in the Labour Party leadership). How can those who acquiesced in the despatch of Diego Garcians to Mauritius, where they would predictably languish in an alien environment to create an Anglo-American fortress, possibly wax righteous about the paramountcy of islanders' views?

Cecil Woolf and Jean Wilson's second question must be answered twice—once in terms of what I would have done, had I been British Foreign Secretary on 2nd April 1982 and, secondly, what I could do at the time of writing, 10th June 1982, since every life lost, on either side, renders a permanent solution more difficult.

It is easy to be wise after the event, but in my case, I 'phoned John Silkin's personal assistant on Friday, 2nd April to express alarm that as Labour's Defence Spokesman he had gone on the 'World at One' and allowed himself to be cornered by the interviewer into committing my party to the use of force. The next day, Saturday, I arrived at the Commons early to tell colleagues, like George Foulkes MP, that I was horrified at our party's stance. Though I interrupted Mrs Thatcher's opening speech to ask her whom she thought her friends in South America were on this issue, I was not called to speak in the hysterical three hours in which the Commons despatched the task force. On 4th April I outlined to West Lothian Constituency Labour Party what should be done, rather than send the 'most ill-conceived expedition to leave our British shores since the Duke of Buckingham set sail for La Rochelle in 1627'.

I would myself, as Foreign Secretary, have gone to Buenos Aires, accompanied not only by senior diplomats but by the Director of the British Antarctic Survey, Dr Lawers, together with a number of eminent geophysicists and marine biologists and would have said to General Galtieri:

'You would not expect us to say that we approve of the military landing in the Falklands/Malvinas. But, you know and we know that military action would be out of all proportion to any argument between us. Further, we know and you know, that talk of economic sanctions is preposterous in a situation where your neighbours, like Brazil, for the past 149 years have officially recognised the Malvinas as part of Argentina and would be happy to help you evade sanctions. Other than a skirmish with Paraguay, you have never fought a war and there has been a history of friendship between our two countries ever since we helped you become independent of Spain.

'Frankly, we are not at all clear what the position of the Malvinas is, in international law. We concede that in the 1830s Britain did take the Malvinas from the Spanish Empire and there were the dubious activities of Samuel Lafone and others. Our Foreign Office knows of some embarrassing documents, which purport to uphold the claim of Argentina, and we concede that the authoritative work on the subject *The Struggle for the Falklands* by the American academic Jules Goebel (1927) comes down on the Argentinian side of the argument, on the basis of the doctrine of *uti possidetis*, recognised throughout Latin America.

'So, President Galtieri, in the knowledge that you have many pressures on your home front, which prompted you to jump the gun in the takeover of the Malvinas—it was going to happen anyway—and in the knowledge that your Junta shows signs of trying to do something for the "disappeared ones", the victims of preceding governments, we should like to put three requests to you.

'First, will you allow those English-speaking people, some of whom we admit are second-class citizens of the UK under our Nationality Acts, to have the same rights, in relation to language and culture, as the Scottish and rugger-playing Welsh communities of rural Argentina?'

The answer would have been, 'Of course, Foreign Secretary, they shall have the same rights. Since there are no roads outside Port Stanley and you have been unable to find the £12 million for infrastructure suggested by your 1976 Shackleton Committee, we think driving on the left or right-hand-side of dirt tracks is not a momentous issue. Nor do we think it a great hardship to instruct the young in the Spanish language since many of them come to school in Buenos Aires, or come here for hospital treatment.'

'Secondly, President, there are some—possibly a few— who will wish to leave the islands. Can we agree on some fair compensation terms?'

'Yes we can agree that anyone who wants to leave is

free to do so. But we must point out that your Shackleton
Committee found that one-quarter of the farms and 46%
of the land is externally owned, much of it by people in
the pressure group called the Falkland Islands Company.
This is owned by Coalite, who have won over a number of
your MPs. People who are more English than the English
ought to have their home in the Thames Valley, where
they spend most of the year in any case. We can work
something out on compensation. However we will
distribute land to those who remain who until now have
been little more than company serfs, dependent on the
Company for their livelihood.'

'Thirdly, President, are you willing to guarantee the
work of the British Antarctic Survey and the well-being of
the scientists? Further could we not extend scientific co-
operation between Argentina and Britain in the
sub-Antarctic? We would point out to you that many
Argentinians have distinguished themselves at British
universities and indeed your César Milstein at the MRC
Laboratories in Cambridge led the team that developed
the enormously important monoclonal antibodies. Now I
have Dr Lawers and his colleagues here. Perhaps they could
discuss an agreement? We know that the Malvinas are an
extension of the South American continental shelf, but
you know that South Georgia and the South Sandwich
Islands are geologically different. None the less we ought
both to put our minds to the winning of resources by the
signatories of the Antarctic Treaty.'

In early April, the answer in Buenos Aires would have
been 'Delighted. We look forward to doing battle with you
in the World Football Cup in Spain'.

With a minimum of leadership and political guts such a
solution could easily have been sold to the British public,
most of whom would have been hard pressed to tell one
where the Falkland Islands were on the map. For Argentinians the Malvinas are an integral part of their country.

Ten ghastly weeks later, Friday, 11th June 1982. Young
men are reported as jumping into the sub-Antarctic sea

with appalling burns. Many young lives have been sacrificed.
Each drop of blood spilled makes a permanent solution
more difficult.

Some years ago I read Cecil Woolf and John Bagguley on
Vietnam — with embarrassment, since I had not been one
of Labour's Vietnam rebels and wished that I had stopped
being the late Richard Crossman's Parliamentary Private
Secretary in order to add my voice to criticise the Government's endorsement of US policy. Now there is the haunting
thought that the Falklands could provide a British Vietnam
in the South Atlantic. What happened to the Americans in
Vietnam was that the fighting, in spite of their military-
technological 'victories' went on, and on, and on. They got
'stuck there'. *Our British problems in the South Atlantic
will just begin when, and if, we 'win'.* For Argentina is not
going to give up her claim to the Malvinas. The Galtieri
government may or may not fall. What is clear beyond
peradventure is that any possible government of Argentina,
right, centre or left, military or democratic, is not going to
surrender its claim to the Malvinas. This is the unpalatable
truth that we all have to face.

As of 11th June I fear that the Prime Minister and her
Defence Secretary are launching themselves into a situation
from which our country will find it difficult to escape. As
with the Americans in Vietnam, the Falklands war is a
process, to which for Britain there can be no favourable
outcome.

Since 3rd April, when I said publicly that no vessel ought
to leave Portsmouth harbour, I have called for the return
of the task force. Embarrassed though they may be, our
leaders will have to accept that sooner or later they will
have to do just this. The sooner it is done the better.
How much of the package that would have been available
to us on 2nd April will still be available, depends on how
soon we bow to the inevitable and recognise the folly of
this ludicrous and unnecessary expedition. What began as
comic opera, became farce, turned into an episode in
British history and is now a raging calamity.

Margaret Drabble

'Patriotism,' said Dr Johnson, 'is the last refuge of a
scoundrel.' It might also be said to be the last refuge of
unhappy governments, and one of the things that most
depressed me in the miserable Falklands business was the
spectacle of the British Public being encouraged by the
government and pro-government journalists to indulge in a
fervour of patriotic sentiment. The same things was happening in Argentina, which didn't make the British response
any more edifying. In this country, the Falklands crisis was
a good way of forgetting unemployment at home, and
forging a kind of national unity through rhetoric. But how
spurious a sense of unity time will surely prove it to have
been, inspired as it was by so inadequate a cause. At the
moment, in the aftermath of victory, people according to
the polls seem to believe that this escapade will have raised
Britain's status in the eyes of the world. They cannot have
been paying much attention to foreign news over the past
few weeks. The whole affair seems to have been an embarrassment rather than a triumph: a 'famous victory' of the sort
that Southey recorded in his lines on the battle of Blenheim.
I am patriotic enough in what I hope is a less escapist way
to have found it deeply embarrassing. We were repeatedly
asked to 'rejoice' over an affair that would not have
happened at all had Britain taken its responsibilities to the
Falklands more seriously in the past, and to congratulate
ourselves on a principled stand that everyone knows we
would not have dared to take on a more dangerous issue.
The complacency with which we were originally told that
the defeat of the Argentines would be a 'walkover', the
change of tone when it was found that many lives would be
lost, were both equally distressing. The arrogance with
which we spoke of the United Nations was a disgrace. And
the enjoyment which so many clearly derived from the
warfare, from a safe distance, is to nobody's credit. Bread
and circuses, I kept thinking, as I watched yet more news-
reel, yet more *Boy's Own* drawings of battleships. The

Falklands war was fought to satisfy wounded national pride, and that doesn't seem to me a good enough reason for 1,000 dead. We claim that we have taught the world that aggression doesn't pay. It seems unlikely that we have done anything of the sort. I shall watch with interest for the moment in the history of world conflict when Britain's heroic stand over the Falklands inspires any other nation with a sense of international duty, responsibility and solidarity. I think it is more likely to go down in history as one of the most pointless conflicts ever, a kind of frenzied outburst of dying power, a misplaced archaic and vainglorious adventure which serves only to emphasize the fact that our role as a world power is over. We make ourselves ridiculous. 'We'? Well, yes, we, for we are all British, but there must be a better way of being British than this.

I don't wish to imply that I'm defending the Argentinians. I'm not. But there must have been other ways, diplomatic ways of solving such a business in the twentieth century. When Mr Healey suggested that a time might come when more might die in the fighting than lived on the Falklands I thought he was making a black joke, but as it turned out he wasn't far wide of the mark. There are presumably those who argue that a ratio of five thousand dead for fifty islanders would have been acceptable, principle being what it is, and I am no doubt one of those who, according to the leader writers of the *Daily Telegraph*, maunder on about the so-called sanctity of human life, in a cowardly and unpragmatic manner. I do in fact believe in the sanctity of human life, foolish though the concept may seem to some, but I'm not a total pacifist. There are issues on which I think it possible that I might think it necessary to fight. But this was so far from being one of them that I think we as a nation stand condemned for lack of judgement, proportion, statesmanship. We won, with more difficulty than we anticipated, a very small war that need never have been fought. It is not an occasion for national rejoicing. I'd rather we won the World Cup. The emotions unleashed by that are relatively harmless. And in point of fact, it is

slightly cheering that there hasn't been much national rejoicing. A depressed nation enjoyed the drama of watching others play battleships, as they enjoyed the drama of the siege of the Iranian embassy, but at least they have the sense not to walk about the streets waving Union Jacks.
21 June 1982

Richard Eberhart

I am for your government's response to the Argentine annexation of the Falkland Islands. Britain did the West a favor by standing against such wicked conduct and I hope your response to this junta, which represses its own people, will notify other juntas, if and when they appear, that civilized nations will not tolerate the Falkland kind of evil doing.
17 June 1982

H.J. Eysenck

I think the British government's response to the Argentine annexation of the Falkland Islands was entirely justified, and executed with exemplary determination, courage and competence. Unless one is willing to allow aggressively-minded countries to upset the *status quo* by invasion and other warlike activities, one has to support the authority of the United Nations' condemnation of such a step by force of arms.

To say this should not disguise from us the fact that the responsibility for not having dealt with the problem earlier must lie with several British governments which failed to come to a peaceful understanding with Argentina. It might surely have been cheaper to have given each inhabitant of the Falkland Islands a pension of £20,000 a year, and bought them villas in any part of the world where they might have wished to go, rather than face a much greater expenditure of money and, much more important, of lives now. Legal rights in colonial possessions are doubtful at best, but physical propinquity is not.

This fact should suggest a resolution of the dispute, ultimately handing over the islands to the Argentinians. The fact of their aggression and the shedding of blood on both sides makes such a solution impossible for a very long time, and perhaps the best that can be hoped for is that the islands would be held by the United Nations in some form of trusteeship, with the consent of the islanders themselves. Whether that is feasible it is not possible to tell at the moment, and the emotions engendered by the 'war' will make any rational or reasonable solution of the conflict difficult if not impossible. That is the tragedy produced by the aggression of the Argentinian junta; we can only hope that one positive outcome of it will be the reluctance of others to follow in their footsteps.

Ian Fletcher

I do not support the general policies of the present Government. I do support their response to the Argentine annexation of the Falkland Islands. There seems no reason why 1,800 people living very much more sanely than most others: no crime, very few roads and so few cars, no television, etc. should be driven out of their own land and forced to live under an oppressive South American dictatorship. The Argentines have no claim to the islands. The Falklanders have as much right to the islands as the Americans have to the USA. Direct negotiations with the Argentines seem to have got nowhere. Here, the Argentines have some right on their side since they seem to have been misled by the Wilson government into believing that their claim to the islands would be granted; ably seconded in this by the hordes of Foreign Office officials at home and abroad.

The alternative to force is the use of the United Nations. But that piece of absurdist theatre can hardly be taken seriously. Its resolution has been ignored. Moreover, the response of the Third World remains all too predictable. The magic word 'colonialism' has only to be uttered for everyone at once to stop thinking and indulge in ritual howls.

As to what happens after the fighting, that is less clear. The Falklanders may recognise that the horrors of the modern world are inescapable and so opt to return to the north-west of Scotland or to try the South Island of New Zealand. If that proves the case, they should be bought out by the Argentines at a generous rate. The way will then be clear for international exploitation of the food resources of the seas, etc. If the Falklanders do not wish to leave, then the Brits will have to maintain forces and themselves exploit the area. If there is to be any role for Argentina, it should be as part of an international enterprise.

12 June 1982

Peter Fryer

The Falklands war enabled both governments to divert public attention from real problems. In the case of the British government the chief of these problems are mass unemployment and the Irish war. Both historically and in international law Argentina has, no doubt, a well-founded claim to the Falklands. But compared with the real problems facing humanity, which set of robbers controls a tiny bit of land in the South Atlantic is a pseudo-problem. That such a pseudo-problem should have led to hundreds of young men being sent to their deaths by elderly politicians is outrageous. The only real solution to the Falklands dispute, and to many real problems, would be the removal

of both governments and their replacement by people
capable of applying reason to human affairs. I am afraid
that will not happen soon; nor will it happen without a
struggle.
16 June 1982

Raymond Garlick

Writers of Wales, whether in Welsh or English, are likely to
have a distinctive attitude to the Falklands situation. Since
1865 there has been a Welsh settlement in Patagonia, in the
southern Argentine, originating in oppression by British
Conservative landlords in Wales at that time. The settlers
became citizens of the Argentine Republic but preserved
their Welsh way of life. Contacts between Wales and the
Welsh settlement have remained close. Patagonian Welshmen
and women continue to come to Wales (bilingual in Welsh
and Spanish, but with no English), and Welsh people to
visit Patagonia. The Argentine view that the Falklands were
annexed by British aggression in 1833 is thus not a strange
one in Wales. The present conflict, the sending of the Welsh
Guards to the Falklands and the presence of Welshmen
among the crews of the ships, raised the possibility that
Welshmen from Wales would be confronting Welshmen from
Patagonia (as has indeed happened). For these reasons, as
well as because it is committed to non-violence, Plaid
Cymru (the Welsh National Party) protested to the London
Government about the sending of a military expedition to
the Falklands. The Welsh TUC, Welsh miners, the Welsh
Council of Churches, have also done so. This in no way
implies indulgence towards the Argentine junta, supplied
with weapons and the skills of violence until recently by
the British Government—thus achieving the deaths, among
many other victims, of Welshmen on both sides.
     Violence at any level—personal, communal, national,
international—is barbarism. It is said that last year's riots

in the great English cities were motivated by a passionate
desire for justice, civil rights, self-determination; but the
violence was rightly condemned. Now the British Government itself, allegedly motivated by the same ideals, has set
an example of international violence. We do not yet know
what grave consequences this may have—both for our
planet and for these already too violent little Isles.

For myself, my father was wounded in the First World
War and many of my friends were killed in the Second. I am
appalled that men and women of my generation, in London
and Buenos Aires, are still prepared in 1982 to send other
people's sons to kill and maim each other in the South
Atlantic. I am appalled at the sanctimoniousness and
violence of British nationalism, the warmongering of most
of the English tabloid newspapers, the attacks on free and
reasoned speech and the BBC, the virtual collapse of
democratic opposition in Parliament. I am grateful to the
thirty or so Socialist and Plaid Cymru Members of
Parliament who have attempted to ensure that the voice of
reason and civilization is heard—and also (though a
secular humanist) to the Roman Pontiff for the same.

The solution? Perpetual exile on the Falklands Islands for
both Argentine and British juntas and their most trident
supporters, there among the graves of their young victims
to begin to learn together the elements of being adult,
rational, civilized human beings.
4 June 1982

David Gascoyne

On returning yesterday (7 June 1982) from a five-day trip
to Paris, I found your questionnaire awaiting me. Fortunately the time at present at my disposal for answering the
two very clear-cut questions to which you request an
answer is limited, since the whole Falklands issue has been
for me personally from the outset murky, to say the least,

and I should otherwise have been tempted to run on in my usual prolix fashion, trying to make clear the least nuances of my reaction. Had I been asked to reply either to the questionnaire regarding the Spanish Civil War, or that sent out by you in 1966 to elicit reactions to the war in Vietnam, my answers would have been brief and categorical. I hope and trust my left-wing principles have not become woolly with the passing of time, but concerning what is at this moment taking place in the S. Atlantic, I still find myself in a to a certain extent divided state of mind, although my initial reaction, during at least the first three weeks of the conflict, was one of cold, simmering fury. The keyword I would have then chosen as preeminently applicable to our unvigilant government's reaction to the Argentine's take-over of what the French, for instance, have always known as *les Malouines*, was 'ineptitude', a term I should still precede with the qualification 'colossal'.

Living in the Isle of Wight as I have now for many years, I had been for some time not altogether unaware that just across the Solent, at Southampton, an Argentine office was established with the express purpose of purchasing arms from us, something which they apparently continued to do without the least difficulty up until less than two months before the junta's attack; nor, as has been pointed out by allegedly seditious spokesmen, did any government official then ever make any reference to the detestable nature of repressive Latin American regimes, certainly not to the blatantly fascist Argentine one. All such regimes, no doubt, were tacitly regarded as providing at least a temporary check to the ever-lurking threat of Soviet-inspired sub-version. The scandal of the debilitated laxness of our once much-vaunted Intelligence Service is too obvious to mention. The muscle-flexing televised announcements of just what we were intending to do and just how we would carry out our intentions with which during the latter half of the second month of the conflict the BBC and, possibly more moderately, ITN regaled us appeared flagrantly to contra-dict the maxim with which we were once so familiar,

according to which dangerous talk costs lives, and were
tantamount to releasing information one would have
considered surely to be classified as secret to the world at
large and especially, of course, to the doubtless highly
gratified Argentines' vigilant Intelligence Services.

Here I must admit that, although initially much in
sympathy with the stand, now seen never to have stood a
chance, adopted by Tony Wedgewood Benn and Dame
Judith Hart, there came a moment when whatever residual
element of 'pragmatism' remains ingrained in my outlook
told me that once this 'unfortunate adventure', as even the
most sympathetic elements of the French press have more
than once qualified it, was embarked on, involving the
impulsive despatch of as massively imposing a task force as
we could muster, then it was simply futile to continue
insisting on the pursuit of 'international negotiations' under
the umbrella auspices of the UN, so patently stuck in
interminable sessions of confused blah blah predestined to
checkmate. Not without some reluctance, I yielded to what
has surely been a very widespread feeling: now that our
government's operations have irrevocably started, let's get
the whole thing done with as fast as possible, with the
minimum of bloodshed and loss of life on both sides.
Yesterday evening's BBC 'Newsnight' programme, however,
undertook a discussion of the serious possibility of a
prolonged war of attrition. 'If only the Argentines,'
observed a typical military interviewee, 'would have the
decency to call it a day and lay down their arms, many
lives might still be saved'; yet he seemed realistic enough
to be prepared to admit they would be unlikely to behave
in so conveniently gentlemanly a fashion.

Despite having been all my life of a resolutely left-wing
political tendency, I think I may justly claim also to have
been since coming of age properly patriotic. I should be
proud to think that my kind of patriotism might be considered not dissimilar to that of my friend the late
Humphrey Jennings. Perhaps my favourite London statue
is that of Nurse Edith Cavell in the Charing Cross Road,

with inscribed at its base her terse last words: 'Patriotism
is not enough'. Unfortunately our national idea of decency,
admirable though it may be, is not now enough either.
Though we now know Dr Johnson's dictum to the effect
that patriotism is the last refuge of scoundrels to have
been too often misquoted, surely true love of one's country
is rather something that entails lucid auto-criticism and
the desire to be able to be honestly proud, without
complacency or chauvinist self-deception, of the genuinely
good characteristics and actions of the nation into which
one happens to have been born. Though probably the
majority of French people, for instance, still consider our
counter-offensive against Argentina to have been funda-
mentally justifiable, and many are obviously embarrassed
by the French origin of the execrated exocet, at least one
reputable daily paper has drawn attention to the tendency
of our media to exaggerate (*gonfler*) the least (*les plus
minces*) details concerning adolescent Argentinian vandalism
and seemingly arrogant cockiness, and to a certain
repetitious self-righteousness in our communiqués. This is
not to suggest that the reports and propaganda emanating
from Buenos Aires are not immeasurably more mendacious
and distorted than our own; but one would wish there to
be observable a total contrast between the treatment of the
continually changing situation by the press controlled by a
typical fascist military dictatorship and its reporting as
undertaken by those purporting to give voice to the views
of a true democracy. To someone like myself, who for at
least fifty years has tried, in however insignificant or ineffectual a way, to further international understanding and
the recognition of European cultural unity, the risk we now
run of alienating our continental neighbours by adopting a
course of behaviour that might only too easily be mistaken
for a reversion to the casual superiority and unquestioning
self-assurance typical of our empire-building colonialist
era at its apex is, to put it mildly, perturbing.

  Another question raised by the present conflict that is
closely connected with the factitious patriotism too

frequently encouraged by our media is that concerning the compassion most sections of society naturally feel for the young men who have lost or are still risking their lives in atrocious conditions very far from home, 'in the cause of freedom', as most of them no doubt keenly believe, and as we must all trust they will eventually turn out in fact to have been doing. When President Reagan seeks to reassure us that what they are fighting for down there is not 'real estate' but rather the noble cause of demonstrating that aggressive invasion of territory will always meet with in-flexible resistance, it is difficult for anyone with a retentive sense of the history of this century not to remember the quasi-sacred principle that took the form of our duty to defend brave little Belgium against the unprovoked aggression of the last of the Kaisers in 1914, a cause that led vast numbers of young men to lay down their lives for it with enthusiasm, while ten years later an equally vast number of survivors came to regard their sacrifice as having been futile and vain. How long will it be this time before people will sadly or bitterly be wondering 'where have all the flowers gone?' The natural compassion just alluded to, moreover, is apt to be modified in the most detrimental way if one draws a parallel with, for instance, the recent utterances of M. Georges Marchais when he seized the obvious opportunity to denounce the 'imperialist powers' for once more using the young men at their disposal as 'cannon fodder', especially if one happens to be aware that this political leader not long ago caused such offence by his unmistakably antisemitic remarks that numbers of his most intelligent followers resigned from the Party of which he remains the head. Opportunism of this description has recognisable counterparts here; but wherever it manifests itself it is at the present time doubly dangerous because it is so apt to encourage the apathetic disillusionment with *all* political parties and their actions that would appear to represent today the gravest danger facing what we believe to be authentic democracy.

During my brief recent stay in Paris, I was fortunate

enough to have the opportunity of conversing for an hour or so with a distinguished writer (one of *les Quarante* in fact) whose name I have no inclination to drop but whose love of our country and most things English is among his marked characteristics. He declared himself grieved and concerned by the situation in which the British find themselves at the moment, but more particularly anxious about the long-term outcome of the conflict, whatever that may turn out to be. He also expressed to me the view, with which, though a younger and less privileged observer, I find myself wholly in accord, that the bleakest factor in all public affairs today is the absence of any figure of sufficient stature to inspire wholehearted international admiration and confidence, the ubiquitous presence, in other words, of seldom more than mediocre representative officials. Incompetence in diplomacy, in strategy and in statesmanship appear to have become endemic in the field of international relations. Is it not also astonishing how few supposedly responsible British politicians appear to have more than the most elementary notion of the nature of the Latin-American temperament with its legitimate idiosyncrasies, all contributing to the varied but closely related cultural traditions of those countries originally colonized by Spain and Portugal? It seems to me not entirely irrelevant to speculate how many of the public men who have been most vocal during the past sixty or so days are at all familiar with the works of Conrad, Hudson or Cunningham Graham, for instance. Even some acquaintance with the writings of Prescott would surely assist the development of some degree of understanding of the historical background of that part of the Western hemisphere that has lately been brought to the forefront of world attention.

At this point, realising that despite having written about the subject of your questionnaire at inordinate length I do not appear to have taken any definite stand with regard to it, I must quench my explanatory verbal flow. Just in case you should find, understandably enough, that this contribution to your dossier is too long to print as it stands,

I now append a short poem which you might care to use in place of the preceding pages. It was hastily written on the day mentioned in the title and revised the day after. The rather feeble intended pun contained in the title refers to the quite insignificant fact that I have seldom written what are generally known as 'occasional poems'. It is clearly a non- or apolitical poem, and is distanced from the burning Falklands issue by the use of a deliberate form, which is that of a verbal square made up of 144 syllabic units, as follows:

Rare Occasional Poem
May 13th 1982

The 'Thought for the Day' that was broadcast this morning
Told us Crisis means Judgement. But who is the Judge?
You may or may not feel that one can exist.
Judgement can signify verdict, decision or
Fate, among other things. Yesterday, Fatima:
Priest tried to stab Pope. There was one more announcement
That a new Incarnation of Christ will appear
On TV before June has ended; by which time
Perhaps the dense fog which at present surrounds us
Will have somewhat dispersed, thus revealing at least
Whether fervour for fatherland, freedom or force
Have prevailed in the South Atlantic, — or foresight.

Stella Gibbons

I leave opinions on public affairs to wiser heads.
    I want, *passionately*, that *no-one* shall be hurt or killed in the Falklands affair.
6 June 1982

Penelope Gilliatt

This war should never have happened; it takes two to make a
fight and we could have found a way without fists. The deep
anxiety is that the Tory Government under Mrs Thatcher
appeared to be acting for the whole nation, and in a spirit of
tantrum. This is not the age of the Crimea. A tantrum can
blow the planet to smithereens. The repercussions of British
Tory action have already been appalling. Mrs Thatcher told
us that we could have gone on arguing for ever. But better
to argue forever than to die or kill forever.

And *why*? People ask that the world over. Oil? The
putative mineral riches of Antarctica? Ransack this earth
for greed? We could have taken care of the 1,800 electively
British Falkland islanders by evacuation. We *must* invent
and support a form of world government that can emerge
from the UN and stop comparing it with the League of
Nations: feeble of our species to call this, our chief hope,
fatuous, for only we make it so.

A (Falkland) island is a small piece of land entirely
surrounded by advice.
21 June 1982

Rumer Godden

While, like T.S. Eliot, I feel writers should remain isolated
from taking part in politics, it seems to me the quarrel is
founded on the now only too common 'grab and greed'
(on both sides) and that the real villains were those long
ago people who first ran up the Union Jack on those
faraway islands and encouraged British people to go and
settle there. However, Britain having got herself in that
position had no option but to defend it. Now having
achieved that, I cannot imagine what the outcome will be
but it would seem a joint protectorate, England and
Argentina, would be best.
16th June 1982

Christopher Hampton

I am totally against it. By sending a massive force of ships and men armed with the most sophisticated weapons – 'a task force of prodigious power', as the Chairman of the Conservative Party puts it – to the South Atlantic, and thus asserting the murderous logic of war as an instrument of policy, the British Government reacted to the crisis in the worst spirit of aggressive nationalism, and demonstrated its clear contempt not only for the authority of the United Nations but also for the civilizing principles of justice without which all nations must sink back into barbarism. There is no way that this profoundly regressive resort to military action can be made to serve the cause of peace and progress in the world, let alone the rights of the oppressed. For even if the original annexation of the Falkland Islands is to be defined as an act of illegal aggression perpetrated by an unpalatable 'Fascist' Junta, the argument that 'aggression doesn't pay' is not to be supported by defying legality and launching 'a long and bloody campaign' of retaliation which compounds and escalates the aggression. We have to remember that it was only after fruitless negotiations, treated as peripheral by Mrs Thatcher and her colleagues – though at the same time the Junta was being openly encouraged to buy British arms (including missiles, planes, guns, bombs and ships) for Argentina – that Galtieri decided to act. Having already gauged the temper of the people over a deeply emotive and popular issue, he at least accomplished the invasion almost without bloodshed; three Argentinians died and not a single islander was harmed. But the first major action of the British task force, apart from the bombing of Stanley airport, was the sinking of the *General Belgrano* in Argentinian waters, 35 miles outside a unilaterally imposed exclusion zone and 200 miles away from (and thus no threat to) the nearest British ships – an act of aggression difficult to justify under any circumstances (and certainly not in the midst of delicate peace negotiations), which caused the deaths of at least 320 men and made nonsense of the Cabinet's claim that Britain (in contrast to Argentina) 'has shown all the restraint of a strong and civilized nation'. Since when, in the battles of the East Falklands, hundreds more have died, and the final death-count of this war could well exceed the total population of the Islands — 250 of them British, the rest Argentinian; though of course for us the Argentinians hardly count. And what were these men sacrificed for? It seems to me they died in the service of the doctrinaire interests of two reactionary powers, each risking itself to divert attention from repressive policies pursued against their own people at home, and intent on gaining maximum political advantage from the crisis.

Now that Mrs Thatcher's gamble, her Government's opportunist exploitation of the crisis, built upon propagandist appeal to the crudest forms of nationalistic sentiment and at immense cost in resources, has paid off with the handsome dividend of military success, it will be used as a weapon to re-inforce Tory political strategy against the unemployed and the disadvantaged and to extend its repressive 'law-and-order' manipulation of the economy. For there is little doubt that the strengthening of military and police powers, the constant wrecking tactics aimed at stripping back and breaking up the community services, and above all the belligerent policy of support for the nuclear arms race (US bases in Britain, Cruise and Pershing, the recent decision to go ahead with the Trident missile system) and a general upgrading of militarism, are all consistent with the aggressive dogmatism that launched such an ostentatious armada of death-ships upon the Falklands.

The dispute is going to have to take into account the ambiguous nature of the issues involved — the question of the sovereignty of the Islands vis-a-vis (1) the long-standing claims of Argentina as a country with an extended history of colonialist exploitation by both Britain and the US, and (2) the dubious right of the British as a colonial and once-

imperial power to retain control of a colony seized by
force 150 years ago. And these issues can only be resolved
by serious negotiation between the disputing parties.

However, such negotiation cannot be meaningfully
pursued so long as the so-called liberal democracies
continue to exploit the poorer countries of the world by
operating through an economic system dominated by
powerful monopolies intent on keeping the people repressed
and subordinate. According to one British Conservative,
Alan Clark, victory in the Falklands means first and fore-
most the prospect of more buyers on the arms market.
'The only world opinion that counts,' he says, 'is the one
that queues up to buy the kit you've won with.' Not a
hint of concern for the rights and needs of people, let
alone their survival. Competitive success in the war for the
market product is all that matters. And in these terms the
weak must go to the wall.

But reason and sanity demand that we reject such callously
inhuman procedures. Either we stand for international co-
operation and world peace, a socially productive economic
system which functions to the advantage of the dispossessed
millions of the Third World, or we surrender our rights and
freedoms to the laws of armed force and repressive order
which at present dictate the policies of the dominant powers,
and which at immense cost in resources are turning that
world into a vast arsenal of genocidal weapons for the
destruction of the human race.

Mrs Thatcher's victory in the Falklands is a victory for
the enemies of the English people, for the militarists and
the arms merchants, those who would seek (as they have
done so often in the past) to hedge the land round with
restrictive laws to enforce conformity and obedience upon
us against the natural laws of justice, equity and reason.
17 June 1982

Tim Heald

It has been a wretched business and watching from the
other side of the Atlantic there has seemed something
rather disgusting about Mrs Thatcher's political fortunes
being revived in such a way. It is one thing to recognise the
necessity of going to war but quite another to take pleasure
in it. The Argentine invasion of the Falklands left the
Government with no alternative. They were right to send
the task force though I would have liked us to have tried
harder to work out some sort of agreement with the
Secretary General of the UN's mediation. In the long term
it makes no sense to maintain the islands as a British
possession in the face of Argentinian opposition. We have
to negotiate a settlement. If Argentina had the sort of
government which anyone—islanders or negotiators—
could trust this shouldn't be too difficult; but the war
hasn't made it any easier and there is no sign of the
Argentinians introducing the sort of society in which the
Falklanders might be prepared to live. There is an almost
exactly parallel situation in the North Atlantic where the
islands of St Pierre and Miquelon, just off the Newfound-
land coast, remain a part of the French Republic. This is
not particularly satisfactory for the French or the
Canadians but because Canada is a sane democracy they are
highly unlikely to precipitate a crisis by invading the islands.
There can only be a satisfactory solution when the Argentinians put their house in order.
16 June 1982

Patricia Highsmith

I am in favour of England's decision to fight in response to
the Argentinian annexation of the Falklands, as a matter
of principle. But I regret the loss of life, of ships, and the
expense that will follow for England to maintain this

principle. Should the world admire and be grateful to England for showing us that not every country can walk into another's piece of land, however small, with impunity? Perhaps. I do not forget, nor should the world, that England was the first to declare war on Germany after the invasion of Poland in 1939. There would not be so many little wars today, if other countries had similar pluck, or if the United Nations had an army capable of defending boundaries established by international law. More interesting will be to learn the opinions, on this same question, of soldiers and sailors who return from the Falklands conflict.
16 June 1982

Christopher Hill

I think it still remains to be explained why the British government allowed the Argentine annexation to happen in the first place; and why they so suddenly discovered that the regime they had been favouring for years was in fact a fascist dictatorship. The government has landed us in an impossible situation by first failing to foresee the annexation and then by launching the task force without adequately considering the implications of their action. As a long-term proposition it is impossible for Great Britain to defend the islands except at fabulous expense. I can see no way out now except by handing the islands over to the United Nations to find some solution which will take account of the interests of the islanders.

If we were totally to abandon nuclear weapons in order to concentrate all our attention on the defence of the Falkland Islands that would be a good bargain. But I fear I do not see that happening.
31 May 1982

Bevis Hillier

At the beginning of the Falklands crisis, which turned into the Falklands conflict, I was annoyed by the failure of British newspapers to give the Argentinian point of view. If I had been an editor, I would have asked an Argentinian (perhaps their Ambassador in London) to contribute an article explaining why his government had acted as it did. I would have given equal space to the opposing British viewpoint.

In the absence of such an Argentinian statement, I had to piece together for myself their justification for invading the Falklands. It seemed to contain three arguments. One was an historical, 'we were there first' argument, which I discounted: on that basis Norway could invade East Anglia because the Vikings were once there. Then there was the 'practical' argument that islands 300 miles from Argentina and 8,000 miles from us should naturally come under their suzerainty, not ours. And Argentina also protested that their government had tried to solve the matter diplomatically for years and had met with nothing but blank obstruction from the British—which left invasion as the only alternative.

These arguments did not convince me. The Falklands were at the time of invasion and are still incontrovertibly ours in international law. Their inhabitants wished to remain British. The Argentines invaded illegally and without warning: it was a Pearl Harbor stunt. They were ordered by the United Nations to get out. They were given seven weeks to do so, and refused, except on terms which would have delivered to them the rewards of their aggression.

In these circumstances I think Mrs Thatcher was right to send the Task Force. And having sent it she was right to agree to no cease-fire not linked to immediate Argentine withdrawal.

I am writing this on 7 June 1982, before the end of the conflict. Who knows how many lives it will cost, on both sides? I regret those lives, and the sufferings of the wounded. It is poignant that the lives have been lost, and the suffer-

ings endured, to regain a few patches of inhospitable land in
the South Atlantic, which in material terms seem hardly
more worth fighting for than Tweedledum's and Tweedledee's
rattle. (Though there is talk of access to mineral deposits
which might be valuable.) But that is not the point.

It *is* a principle at stake—the same principle as was at
stake when Hitler invaded the Sudetenland and Czechoslo-
vakia. Our craven attitude then proved once for all that
appeasement in such circumstances is not only immoral, it
does not pay. (And we note that the Argentine government
is a fascist dictatorship with many aspects in common with
Hitler's, including torture, suppression of a free press, and
the conversion of 'disappear' into a transitive verb. It might
seem odd to find that the left wing, who profess to be
anti-fascist, are utterly feeble when it comes to standing up
to the fascists—until one remembers the fine words of
W.H. Auden and Christopher Isherwood in the 1930s and
their comfortable residence in America when the chance
of fighting Hitler came.)

For the purist pacifists I have far more sympathy, though
I cannot share their attitude. It is logical to oppose the
Falklands fighting if you deplore the shedding of any
human blood. But I remember what Group-Captain
Leonard Cheshire, VC, told me once. He said that when he
was at Cambridge, he and a group of rowdies had gone
round to pacifists' rooms and had demanded £5 from them.
When the pacifists asked 'Why?', Cheshire and his gang had
replied, 'Because if you don't, we're going to beat you up
and throw your furniture through the windows.' In retro-
spect, Cheshire was ashamed of this behaviour, as well he
might be: but as a parable for pacifists it still seems valid to
me.

I admit that even if we take the Falklands, many acute
problems remain—above all, how are we to maintain a
continued defence of the islands against an Argentina of
exacerbated hostility, a wasp which cannot be kept under a
jam-jar for ever? But the principle must be honoured before
the practicalities are attended to. Indeed, it must be

honoured even if they are never satisfactorily worked out, just as governments must refuse to humour hijackers before they work out how to release their captives by force or negotiation. The message to the world from our action in the Falklands is: those who initiate aggression will find it costs them dear and profits them nothing. The message from the pious hand-wringing which Tony Benn and Dame Judith Hart urged on us would have been: grab what you want, it's there for the grabbing.

I would define civilization as that condition of society which militates against the mere survival of the strongest. It is an artificial condition, because, alas, Hobbes was right about human nature—a ceaseless war of man against man. Civilization can only exist if the strong defend the weak against the strong. That is why it was right for us to enterprise an armada against the Argentine invader and to protect the rights of the 1,800 Falkland Islanders.

Mrs Thatcher's decision to send the Task Force, in the face of all kinds of pusillanimity from her own party as well as the Opposition, is a rare example of history not being allowed to repeat itself. One Munich was enough.
7 June 1982

David Holbrook

The main problem which emerges seems to me that of what are we to do about the dynamics of human hate, and its fantasies? This indeed is what a great deal of my own writing has been about, impelled by my own experiences in Normandy as a young man in 1944. The Falklands crisis originated in the collective fantasies of the Argentinians, developed by conscious government policy there, inculcating nationalism. Then, to solve a pressing economic crisis, and to divert attention from its own cruel repressive policies (including mass extermination of opponents) the Junta launched an attack on the Falkland Islands, regardless of the consequences. This kind of thing seems to me to belong to mass psychopathology, whereby the delicate problems of human life and society are solved by machismo, by resort to hate—which really solves nothing, but offers the securities of false pseudo-male strength.

In the face of such an adventure, infringing International Law and the rights of the Falklanders, challenging Britain and her responsibilities, I believe the government's action was right, and the only possible one. The military and naval campaign we have waged seems to me to be a form of 'useful hate', forced upon us by circumstances. It is evident that, if we had not responded as we did, other countries seeking such false solutions might well be encouraged to enter into other enterprises, against weaker countries, or against former colonial powers against which they bear a grudge.

Having said as much, however, another problem emerges, which is that human technology has not advanced so much that it has completely outstripped man's sensibility, and his capacities to know himself, to organise his world, and to deal with such issues. Moreover, commercial trends are such that a vast immoral arms trade pours dreadful weapons into those areas of the world where the most trouble might originate. To this we need to add the problem of *realpolitik* — the cynical manipulation of trouble anywhere, to serve the interests of Russian power, or American interests, or Arab concern, or whatever. In this situation, the hypocrisy of certain countries is unbelievable: what is Cuba, for instance, doing, supporting Argentina, a fascist country? Why is Soviet Russia supplying Argentina with intelligence information? This abandonment of principles is even more dangerous than the tendency towards the solutions of hate.

And as for the British Left! They have responded despicably! Have they forgotten the Spanish War and non-intervention? Have they forgotten the Sudetenland, and appeasement? The working class movement, the socialists, and the radicals should have learnt that there comes a time when fascism must be resisted by force, because the cost of allowing it to get away with its delusions is worse than the cost of standing up to it. It is extraordinary that a conservative government should understand this better than its opponents. The opposition has shown itself devoid of sound insights and principles, by its weakness and shilly-shallying in the face of the problem. Michael Foot's responses, as by his jeers about Mrs Thatcher and her 'boys', have been parochial, confused and mean, and we look in vain for a radical leader in Britain today.

And then one has to add also that this conflict has shown that people are no longer willing to accept the shedding of blood: that they know enough about war to want to develop truly pacifist responses and procedures, to deal with situations of this kind. I believe that when a massive hate-delusion has overtaken a whole people and its leaders, conflict may be perhaps the only solution: but there is hope in the growing genuine pacifism of the mass of the people at large, their disquiet at loss of life, and their desire to pursue truly human solutions. As this movement spreads, perhaps the leaders themselves will be forced to modify their present policies. The success of the terrible exocet missiles shows that, in a nuclear war, many such weapons would get through any form of defence, and so all talk of 'umbrellas' or 'defence' is meaningless, and we must take urgent steps to bring technology within the compass of man's capacities to understand, negotiate, and place limits on his own powers of destruction.
31 May 1982

Michael Holroyd

I am on no side; I am against both. The Argentine invasion of the Falkland Islands was wrong; the British counter-invasion of the Malvinas was also wrong. As we fought it out, braying of patriotism and national prestige, we came every day more closely to resemble each other — which, to judge by what we were saying of each other, was the

last thing either of us wanted. Politically we are still children,
cruel, thoughtless and grandiloquently eager to 'own' or go
adventuring round this almost barren hump of peat and rock.
Has Mrs Thatcher ever seen these islands? Has General
Galtieri? They exist as pebbles in their heads and are no
more worth the calamity of war now than they were over
two hundred years ago when Dr Johnson wrote his *Thoughts
on the late Transactions respecting Falkland's Islands.*
People have been bombed, shot dead, drowned in the
appalling sea. To those alive in both countries, their friends
and loves, I would say they died for absolutely nothing.
That is how terrible the truth is. By pretending otherwise
we may make their deaths seem more acceptable, but we
hand on the baton of untruth for yet another round of
the track. And so it goes.

If we really want to raise our standard of behaviour
above that of the fourth form, we should insist internationally
on what we take for granted in our own country: the best
court of law we can get and an international police force to
take us there whenever we are tempted to break its laws.
7 June 1982

William Douglas-Home

I must confess to some bewilderment over the history of
the Falkland Islands. Both the Argentine and Britain seem
sincerely to believe in their respective claims to sovereignty.
This clouds the issue. One could wish that both would seek
a judgement from some international court. Not to do so,
seems to indicate a lack of confidence. Even a unilateral
approach, if that were possible, from one side or the other,
though it might be nerve-wracking, would clarify the issue,
which would only be to the advantage of the future of the
area.

Though nothing can detract from the achievement of the
forces in the recent war, one wonders whether the direction

of it could not have been less inflexible. By that I mean that UN Resolution 502, combined with sanctions, could conceivably have led the Argentinians to think again. One must confess that they showed little signs of doing so at any stage in the pre-war negotiations, yet it could, perhaps, be argued that the threat of force, which was expected to assist negotiation had precisely the reverse effect. I do not find this utterly surprising since, in my view, force is not the ideal bed-mate for diplomacy. Indeed, it tends to aggravate the situation, whereas sanctions, being less offensive, could be said to run in harness with it. Therefore, it would seem to be a pity that a combination of diplomacy and sanctions was not tried to start with just in case there might have been a moment when the latter started biting hard enough to bring about a change of policy. One must concede, however, that only an optimistic statesman rather than a dedicated politician, would have contemplated taking such a course.

In any case, it was not taken, so the argument is academic. But what happened in the war is very far from being academic, even though it's over. It is also highly relevant as well as being hopeful for the future. And I do not mean the victory, though that was total.

What I am discussing now, with relish, is the way in which conflicting viewpoints were allowed to be aired on the media. Not only by the politicians and the journalists but by the public too. This ventilation, as with every other kind of ventilation, had health-giving qualities. No longer did one suffer from the stultifying atmosphere of World War II, in which a leading and distinguished critic of Sir Winston's policies was called by him, 'a squalid nuisance'.

In this recent conflict, critics were not called such names, just as the US Senators, who criticized the war in Vietnam in public, were not denigrated either.

This is progress, since it means that when the juggernaut of war starts rolling, the brakes can still be applied instead of being, as in most past wars, removed for the duration.

With this innovation, it may not be over-optimistic to

assume that wars, in future, will not have it all their own
way, if a vocal opposition is allowed to function, as in this
most recent one. Admittedly, the Opposition could not
put a stop to this one, but that does not mean it cannot
be done in the future.

Meanwhile, what about the future of the Falkland Islands?
Surely, now the lesson has been taught, however harshly,
that force must not be allowed to supercede negotiation, we
should heed that lesson too. As war is said to be a continuation of politics by other means, so politics should surely
be the continuation of war, which means that we should
start to renegotiate. The argument against this is that those
who died so bravely and so tragically would be insulted. I
profoundly disagree. What they were fighting for was not
a permanent solution imposed by force. Indeed, that is
what they were fighting against. What they were fighting for
was freedom, which should not deny the freedom to
negotiate — to either Britain or the Argentine.
22 June 1982

Michael Horovitz

I'm against most of the British Government's response to
date (9th June), insofar as I've followed what it amounts to.
It looks like hanging on to a colonial outpost of the
ex-British Empire; how talk of 'sovereignty' when the
sovereignhood or reign of the UK by the Royal Family
can't be said to enjoy much real credibility to wave a flag
for anyway? On Prince Charles and Lady Di's wedding
night crowds of teenagers on the last Circle Line tube home
from Kensington were chanting (to the tune of the Cuban
Revolution Santa-Lameda) 'Three Million jobless, and only
One Royal Wedding' . . . some of them probably only had
squats qua homes to go to, let alone any working life-
expectation. If there's no gold in the Sovereign, no silver of
integrity, what use sacrificing hundreds of lives in the name

of non-Empire? Our Iron Battleaxe invoked that rusty old anachronism, her militia, to threaten the bully with a taste of his own medicine. Instead of waiting as long as possible before escalating warfare, and honouring Britain's responsibility as a UN member, she rushed 'her' forces in much sooner than appears to have been advisable on the purely military level, let alone necessary politically.

Fighting over nation-state ownership of bits of land on a planet whose overall survival is now so endangered (see *The Ecologist*'s 'Blueprint for Survival') seems utterly unhistorical. Will it take war with other planets to bring earthlings to their senses?

If the 'EEC' means a truly United States of Europe, linking up with the USA, USSR, the Chinese Republic *et al.* toward a truly United States of the World and of being, I'd work for it—if not fight. Meanwhile instead of refuelling the arms engines, our Government(s) might be better occupied in considering why it is that the United Nations is in fact so frequently divided and why, when their resolutions do occasionally approach unanimity, they so frequently remain ineffectual?

Unhappily, the structure of nation-states we're lumbered with, reinforced by economic demoralisation, cultural philistinism and competitive materialist rat-races, means that Western Governments-elect as well as Police States can 'normally' rely on the herd instinct of their citizens arousing the maximum rabblement—the Lowest Common Denominator of attitudes, including a meanness of spirit, a callousness in regard to the maiming and killing of 'foreigners', and a relative inhumanity to their 'own' people sent to fight—which few of these state-'constituents' or 'herd-units' would care or dare to betray individually, one to another.

How many of the national leaders sending their young men to kill or be killed 'for the flag' would actually rush off and do it themselves? Come off it you nationalists, so quick to give the orders—look at the real inheritances and futures involved and adapt, or surrender . . . the colonial outpost which was under extreme adaptation all along—

but also the global village it could still just continue to be part of.

True, the Argentine Junta had displayed little sympathy with the small-is-beautiful human scale pearl necklace of bits of the earth to be nurtured by friends of the earth; and their assault on the islands was rapacious, and apparently motivated partly to try to retain power and support within Argentina where it's been waning. Thatcher's correspondingly unnecessarily lethal reaction seems to have been partially impelled from similar motives, and has certainly won her administration (and her personally) a certain amount of jingo-istic support against which I hope there will be an incisive backlash. If the bully turns out to seem outbullied it may of course, for a time anyhow, have the reverse effect. But only her most blinkered champions could claim that Mrs Thatcher has proved herself a militant anti-fascist; if she'd been this, she would surely have imposed sanctions against the Junta years ago, and especially would have stopped selling armaments to them. The irony that Argentina's militia are deploying arms and bombs against British troops which were sold to them by Britain is hardly commented on by the most radically committed media, it seems, because the fact of the UK's constantly quietist position in relation to vicious, oppressive and murderous fascist regimes is established and assumed beyond question—until one of them happens to cast a stone in 'our' direction, as distinct from all the others stoned and worse over these years.

If the Second World War of '39-'45 was partly to quell Hitler's genocidal racism, then I agree it was to that extent, a partially just war. The present dispute regarding the Falk-lands is a very different matter. How to resolve it is some-thing no writer could arbitrate on alone, with any justice — it's her autocratic lack of openness to consensus, both within the British political arena and the UN and other worldwide concerns, which sullies any confidence many of us have in the Iron-Thatched stance. What she's invoked is a deadlock—a bunch of sadly brute horns, brutalised against fellow-feeling with their alleged adversaries, locked

with death as the only solution—a course of action which
feeds on itself with potentially endless cycles of destruction
and counter-destruction.

But you ask how the dispute 'should . . . be resolved':
I'd say it *might* move towards a real resolution if representatives of both sides go naked to conference tables—literally,
if necessary. If it took that for most of the governors and
combatants to reveal and recognise their common
humanity—to see it in themselves and each other, that
they're the same being, creature, person—then the absurdity
of mechanised and barbarous acts of violence might be
exposed, and less liable to get promoted again. The words
'negotiated settlement' and 'sovereignty' might be less
operative, and constructive plans for denationalised
occupation of the global homeland start getting drawn up—
and necessarily, respected—overnight—and not just in the
South Atlantic, or Westminster, or the Pentagon or
Kremlin or Peking—but in the Middle East—everywhere.

This will get slagged as 'Utopian dreaming' etc.—soldiers
and marines and bombers have been trained and indoctrin-
ated and conditioned not to care about 'enemies' who
don't 'speak their language' etc, etc. . . . true, partly true,
true too—but NOT *too* true. For those intent on fighting,
those mercenaries conditioned to delight in killing, for
want of other work or purpose, from being incurably
sadistic or psychotic—for whatever reason, could be
allowed to fight one another—but one another ONLY, in
an area of the planet set aside for them to do so where no
one else need get hurt—if enough such committed combatants were found who really wished to proceed with it. But
I'd suggest that initially, any members of armies and the
like given this option be subjected to the following test:
wherever factions are fighting, let there be a brief truce for
say, one night, during which the individual combatants
from both sides who say they wish to go on fighting be
reclothed in anonymous uniforms—that's to say, let all of
them wear the same clothes, and let the individuals then
be reshuffled. So that in the case of the troops currently

engaged around the South Atlantic, of those who chose to go on fighting let half of those who've thus far attacked the British on behalf of Argentina line up with half the Brits, and *vice versa*. When Argentines then get on with murdering their fellow-nationals as well as their 'sworn' enemies, and Britons Britons, perhaps the extreme folly of warfare based on 'the last refuge of a scoundrel' will come home even to any such that are left, who might just then lay down their arms and set about salvaging what's left of this creation.

The degree of mass-murder to which patriotism and authoritarianism have urged so-called humans since Dr Johnson's time is of course almost unspeakable; and it might be relevant to point out that both Britain and Argentina seem, as groups of inhabitants of the globe, in their national constitutions, to take some pride in being not only British and Argentinian, respectively (e.g. socio-cultural groupings of the human species with histories and futurities they are ready to have their citizens fight and die for, as separate groupings); but also in aspiring to a degree of religious or divine consciousness—numerically located in Christianity for the most part, albeit somewhat variegated denominationally. It's unlikely that I need labour the ghastly history of warfare and murder and cruelty that's been perpetrated over the centuries in God's and Christ's names; but isn't it high time—given the now long accomplished fact of worldwide (and even inter-galactic) communications which render Babel an almost prehistoric aside—that loving our neighbours as ourselves were put concretely into practice—and 'our neighbour' understood as absolutely *every* citizen of the world (unless that neighbour is manifestly *not* loving us or himself at all—and there's the rub, some might say, pointing at the Junta and other would-be UNfriendly neighbours. Well, two wrongs don't make a right. Henry Miller in his *Time of the Assassins* wrote fifty years ago, with regret, of 'Modern Man', that '. . . Mentally he is on all fours, and what he fears most —God Pity him—is his own image'. So he, we, resorts to, invoke, these weary complicated webs of would-be insurance, of bluff and counter-bluff, of task forces and alleged deterrents).

Gandhi's style of nonviolent non-co-operation with any warfare, unless as necessary and just as the united front of 1940 against Nazi Germany, seems the least unacceptable solution to me, and especially wherever it can be presented as a genuinely popular mandate—however small a minority might at first seem to be subscribing to it (cf the continuing rise of CND, the far-reaching resistance of the Committee of 100, the supra-national spread of Solidarity, the Greenpeace Movement, Friends of the Earth, *et al.*).

The arms race is crazy by definition, the nuclear one that much more so, and countries such as New Zealand and now a section of Central Wales which seek to opt out would seem the people to collaborate with, setting up more and more nuclear-free peaceloving zones. These may quite soon turn out to be the only bits of earth left worth defending, against ourselves. If they go too, the human experiment may simply be finally burning itself out, as dead an issue as the dinosaur experiment. That would seem exceedingly stupid, a great waste of everything we've built up from B.C. —although in making machines our arm and using our gigantic power like giants, e.g. tyrants, it was more and more the probable culmination. Let's attempt to live up to the positive seeds of humanity still latent, if not always visibly growing, all around and within us. As Gandhi replied when he was asked what he thought of western civilisation: 'I think it would be a very good idea'.

Michael Howard

On our entry into the war I can only say, as George V said to the American Ambassador when Britain declared war on Germany on the latter's invasion of Belgium in 1914: 'Good God, Mr Page, what else could we have done?'

Once entered into the war, we appear to have conducted it with remarkable skill and despatch.

The ultimate justification of the war will have to rest, however, on the peace that we make after it. Neither the British nor the Argentinians are at present in a mood to accept any lasting and sensible solution, and the proposals so far floated have been so many pieces of paper. I am reluctant to add to them. But I see no alternative to some kind of settlement under the auspices of the United Nations, underwritten by the United States.

8 June 1982

P.J. Kavanagh

We were right to mount a suitable force because the law had been broken, and without rules there is no game.

When that force reached the islands and we noticed less than half-hearted support from the world we should have asked, very loudly a question:

Do you believe in the rule of law or not?

In the (certain) absence of a clear reply we should have said:

We do. You don't. We can re-take the islands and restore the law. With your full support it would cost no lives. Without it, there will be deaths, Argentine and our own. In a world without law we do not wish to live but, apparently, we must.

So we will return home, leaving the law successfully broken.

That appears to be your wish.

It is not possible any more for one country to be nanny to the world, though the world still needs one.

16 June 1982

Ludovic Kennedy

Whatever we have come to think about the Falklands affair since it started, we should not forget what we all felt when we heard the Argies had gone in. It was one of outrage, a feeling that national pride had been given a huge dunch, and that the *status quo* should be restored as soon as possible. The House of Commons debate, in which all parties spoke with one voice, reflected the mood of the country.

Later, one came to realise several things. Firstly, that although blame for the invasion lay directly with the Argentine government, our own government were entirely responsible for leaving the place defenceless. Withdrawing the *Endurance* was almost an invitation to the Argies to walk in. Had we left one destroyer or frigate in Port Stanley harbour, I am certain that the Argentines would never have dared to attack.

The history of the place was an eye-opener to me, a confirmation of Proudhon's saying that all property is theft, that aggression does pay and that possession is nine-tenths of the law. Historically and geographically British and Argentine claims would seem to be about equal. We planted a flag on the islands while passing by, but that hardly entitles one to permanent ownership. On the other hand we ran a peaceful administration for 150 years.

Against this the Argentines would claim that they were the first to establish a permanent garrison which we had booted out with superior forces, and that at no time since then had they relinquished their claims to possession; but that the naval and military might of the British Empire had for generations prevented them from ever enforcing those claims. Geographically too, it seems to me, they have a strong case, with the islands lying on the South American continental shelf yet half a world away from Britain.

While the war was on, I was sickened by the jingoism of so many of my fellow countrymen and of so much of the press. This was not a war of national survival, rather the action of a man who finds a burglar in his house and proceeds to eject him. Ejecting a burglar is an unpleasant but necessary task and does not call for war-dances and whoops of joy.

Lastly, if I had had a son killed in the Falklands campaign, I would have had the same sort of regrets as if he had been killed by a burglar — a waste of life caused by my negligence as a householder. We should have made arrangements to transfer the property years ago. Now we are saddled with it, and the expense and bother of defending it, for years. And the Argies, and their claims to it, will always be with us.

23 June 1982

Francis King

I was a pacifist in World War II. But since then I have both lost my faith and learned that, if you offer the other cheek to an opponent, he will usually slap it resoundingly. I am therefore in reluctant support of the Government's response to the Argentine annexation of the Falkland Islands, even though I am mournfully reminded of the soldiers in *Hamlet*

Exposing what is mortal and unsure
To all that fortune, death, and danger dare
Even for an egg-shell . . .

What should be done with the egg-shell, once we have retrieved it, is a problem beyond my abilities to solve. Mrs Thatcher will call on the United States, Mr Foot on the United Nations. We shall certainly have to expend a lot more money on a territory which we culpably neglected for decades.

3 June 1982

James Kirkup

I am a pacifist anarchist, and for that reason totally opposed
to war and any form of violence against either man or beast.

Therefore I abhor the British Government's belligerent
acts in the Falkland Islands. These remote, useless and inhospitable specks of land are not worth the spilling of one
drop of Argentine or British blood. All wars are wars of
aggression and calculated murder, fanned into being by
immoral arms manufacturers and inept politicians. The
outbreak of any war is a failure of diplomacy, and so it is
diplomats, politicians and heads of state who should be
made to pay for them, not the common people. Those
responsible should be stripped of their rank and possessions
and condemned as traitors not only to their own country
but to the entire human race. That Argentina is a despicable
dictatorship intent on destroying the natural rights of man
is beside the point. It takes two to make a war, and so Mrs
Thatcher and her Government are just as guilty as the
Government of Argentina, guilty of murder and bloodshed
and oppression. This ridiculous colonial war of aggression
is a judgment on the idiocy of national pride and ranting
patriotism. It is also an indictment of the total failure of
Britain's economic, spiritual and intellectual life, and a
lapse into nationalistic barbarism.

How to resolve the dispute? Move the Vatican to the
Falklands and let them fight it out with the Pope's Swiss
Guards, and the heads of state of Britain and Argentina.
They would pretty soon reach an agreement. Then the
islands should be abandoned to the birds and beasts who
are their only rightful inhabitants.
5 June 1982

G.R. Wilson Knight

Britain's response to the Falklands crisis was ratified by all
three parties in Parliament, and I accordingly would not

presume to register any complaint. However I feel that behind the astounding speed, energy, resource, expense and brilliant organisation employed in what seems, taking a long view, a hazardous cause, there may be reasons unknown to me and to the general public.

As for the future, I can only assess our prospects by stating my own convictions. I have for long accepted the validity of our country's historic contribution, seeing the British Empire as a precursor, or prototype, of world-order. I have relied always on the Shakespearian vision as set forth in my war-time production *This Sceptred Isle* at the Westminster Theatre in 1941 (described in *Shakespearian Production*, 1964). The theme I also discuss in various writings collected under the title *The Sovereign Flower* in 1958. Our key throughout is Cranmer's royal prophecy at the conclusion of Shakespeare's last play, *Henry VIII*, Shakespeare's final words to his countrymen. This I still hold to be our one authoritative statement, every word deeply significant, as forecast of the world-order at which we should aim. Though democratic, it involves not just democracy alone, but democracy in strict subservience to the crown as a symbol linking love to power and the social order to the divine. For world-order, this symbol, or some adequate equivalent, must be supposed.

It follows that, while respecting its provisional importance as a pool for discussion, I would not regard votes in the United Nations as a safe and final arbiter. Also that I tend to support our activities, now or in the future, in so far as they may be felt to be expanding British tradition and our national heritage to world proportions, in attunement with Shakespearian prophecy.

9 June 1982

Marghanita Laski

Any answer to the second question must, by inference, include one to the first. So I answer the second question, which allows the giving of an opinion rather than the taking of sides where conciliation of views is to be sought.

Military aggression is wrong and should be stopped, and military aggression is what Argentine has committed, a wrong action not comparable to or to be excused by our own failure to make an effective agreement with her earlier.

But I think that the world has reached a position where any one nation's response by war to a wrong committed on itself is, however understandable, as dangerous, and as damaging to any hopes of an international rule of law, as is vigilante action inside the nation-state. I believe our every action in the international field should, before this episode, during this episode, and in the future, be directed towards establishing effective international police action, in which, ideally, the wronged state should not take part. The locusts have eaten the years in which the United Nations might have been willing to act in this way. It is possible that our EEC colleagues, so surprisingly supportive of us over this issue, might have been brought to do so. If no one would have acted collectively on our behalf, then I think it would have been better to have let the Falklands go than to embark on an exercise which has not only caused death and injury, but has evoked a use of jingoistic language and a demand for the suppression of impartial reporting far more damaging to the quality of our national life than the shame involved in making less than ideal arrangements for the Falkland Islanders—though, as *The Times* intimated, the costs of the war divided among the islands' inhabitants might have gone far to have mitigated their loss of this home and their establishment in another.
3 June 1982

Peter Levi

The British Government should have negotiated a solution to the Falklands problem many years ago. I remember a

school debate on the subject in the nineteen forties; the theme was chosen as being attractively obscure and nicely balanced, and the Foreign Office seem to have treated it in the same spirit ever since. I have the impression that they have treated Latin America with arrogant contempt. All this being said, I entirely favour the Government's response to annexation, because the Falklanders have a right to protection, and in this case that means protection by force of arms. I have been a Labour voter since the Suez crisis, because I thought the invasion of Egypt improper, but from now on I shall vote Conservative, because I think the Falkland annexation improper, and rightly to be resisted. You ask how the dispute should be resolved. Of course by negotiation, if and when and in whatever way that may become possible.
1 June 1982

Jack Lindsay

I am totally opposed to the Government's response to the Argentine annexation of the Falklands. As strongly as I disapprove of the military fascist regime in Argentina, its appalling record of murder and torture, and its attempt to seize the islands in order to gain support by seeming to champion the deeply-felt national belief that the islands are Argentinian.

I believe that the islands should have been restored to Argentine when the matter was raised in the postwar period and that our governments, Labour or Conservative, should have realised what a danger-spot they were. That in resisting the seizure our present government is obeying any set of principles I do not for a moment believe. The most superficial glance at our postwar record disproves such a contention. To take only a few examples. Our government without a moment's hesitation threw out the islanders from Diego Garcia and handed the island over to the USA

as a war-base. Though we had troops in Cyprus and should
have upheld the *status quo*, we did not raise a murmur
when the Turks, a military fascist junta, killed many Greeks,
and seized territory. When the Indonesians invaded the
Portuguese colony of East Timor, we did not support any
protest; instead we helped to provide armaments for the
invaders, who have killed, I believe, some 100,000 people.
Without the least question we supplied arms to the Argentinians when it was a matter of building them up as
collaborators with the USA in suppressing popular democratic movements in Latin America. We continue to give full
support to the Turks, members of NATO, who, as I write,
are carrying out a mass-trial of trade unionists, social
democrats, and the like, with demands for the death-
penalty.

It is ludicrous then for our government to invoke any
principle in its policy of regaining the Falklands by force.
In order to relieve Mrs Thatcher of the extreme humiliation
she suffered when the Argentine invasion occurred, the
worst elements in our national tradition have been callously
revived; and it is saddening and alarming that so strong a
popular support has been stimulated.

What then should have been done? It seems to me the
one honourable course was to hand the problem fully over
to the United Nations. Their 502 resolution condemning the
invasion should have been made the basis for a coherent
and largescale series of actions isolating Argentina and
bringing effective economic sanctions and other pressures
to bear upon her. This would have been the correct use of
the resolution, which in no way gave Britain leave to start
her own private war. The argument that the United Nations
is incapable of dealing with such a situation derives from
the fact that the great nations have never sought to use the
organisation consistently and thoroughly. In the present
matter our government has typically denied the UN any
real authority or effective power. Yet here was an excellent
chance to make it a body for effectively enforcing peaceful
and decent behaviour among nations. What has been done

is to weaken yet further the possibility of such a development. There has been no excuse for embarking on such a
bloody war-exercise as the despatch of the task force to
the South Atlantic. The full effects of such a violent course
may well be increasingly disastrous. If such effects can be
curtailed and finally limited, it will certainly not be in any
way due to our government and its choices.
8 June 1982

David Lodge

I was abroad, on holiday in Greece, and out of touch with
news, when Argentina invaded the Falkland Islands, and I
do not know how far I might have shared the feeling of
outrage that seems to have swept the House of Commons,
and most of the country, that fateful weekend. Returning
a week later, and taking stock of the situation after initial
dazed incredulity, I came to the conclusion that we should
not have sent the task force, for the following reasons: 1.
the enterprise was inherently very risky, and the repossession
of the Falklands was not worth the loss of human life,
especially British lives. 2. Even if we were successful in
repossessing the islands, we could never defend them indefinitely against Argentina without an absurdly
disproportionate investment of military capability.

I still hold to the view as I write this, on the 8th June,
with the British forces poised to retake Port Stanley, while
feeling great admiration for the courage and resourcefulness
with which they have conducted the campaign. If there had
to be a war, it is obviously vital that we should win it, since
our cause, it seems to me, is just. Whatever the merits of
the Argentinian claims to sovereignty over the Falklands
(and they are, to say the least, debatable) there was no
need or justification for the junta to assert them at this
particular moment by armed agression. Opponents of the
British Government's policy who brush this consideration

aside, and seek to explain the despatch of the task force as
a last spasm of imperialistic jingoism, or a Tory plot to win
the next election, seem to me to have misjudged the
matter, and certainly the national mood.

Like, I suspect, the majority of my fellow-countrymen, I
feel that the Argentinians committed a wrong. The only
question is: how far should one go in order to right that
wrong? Not an easy question. There is no doubt in my
mind that anything short of Mrs Thatcher's uncompromis-
ing policy would have left the Argentinians at the end of
the day in possession of the Falklands. The catch is that
her policy will probably only succeed in postponing that
day—at the cost of how many lives?

So what would I have done? I would have used our
nuclear submarines, the one weapon we have against which
Argentina seems to have no defence, to impose a blockade
upon the Falklands, and possibly upon mainland Argentina,
to add pressure to economic and diplomatic sanctions. The
Argentinians would, of course, have been able to continue
supplying their garrison by air, but this would have been
costly and inconvenient in the long run. I do not suggest
that the Argentinians would have in fact withdrawn their
forces, but they might have accepted in the end something
less than autonomous sovereignty.

As to the prospects now, I am full of foreboding. Now
that blood has been spilled, neither side can yield on the
basic issue of sovereignty without appearing to render vain
the sacrifice of its servicemen's lives. Unless the US is
willing to bail us out by leasing the Falklands as a military
base—which would almost certainly destroy the Falklanders' way of life that we have fought to defend—there will
have to be either a compromise or arbitration. We cannot
fight Argentine indefinitely, 8,000 miles from our mainland,
and four hundred from theirs. In due course, when passions
have subsided, we should propose taking the sovereignty
issue to the International Court—the verdict not to be
binding on either party, but to provide a basis for further
negotiation. The best solution *would* have been, before the

war broke out, a recognition of Argentinian sovereignty combined with a lease-back of the islands on behalf of the settlers. If this were proposed by a third party it might (just) be acceptable to Britain and Argentina.

Norah Lofts

I cannot approve of armed robbery.

The Argentinian behaviour to *its own people* would make me reluctant to live under that rule myself, or to hand over even the Falkland sheep to their control.

Anything that can be settled by talk can be done in 24 hours. The UN gave one firm ruling which was ignored so that foredoomed negotiations could go on while the weather worsened.

There are reports of the white flag being treacherously used. Napalm has also been mentioned.

Crime must be seen not to pay. And at the end it might not be a bad idea to let our serving men decide the fate of the islands and the islanders.

5 June 1982

Ethel Mannin

I am entirely for it. I don't see how, in the interests of democracy, any other stand could have been taken.

I think the Falklanders should be consulted as to whether they wish to remain under British administration, or opt for independence, self-ruled, though if they choose this they will need British economic help, and a degree of political guidance.

5 June 1982

Julian Manyon

I am wholeheartedly behind Mrs Thatcher's decision to re-
possess the islands by force. In arriving at this position,
even before the fighting actually got under way I was not
really convinced by the public argument that Britain had to
act to deter international agression — this justification
seemed pompous and not a little hypocritical. Instead,
sitting in the Sheraton Hotel, Buenos Aires, as the crisis
progressed from comic opera to full-scale war, there
seemed to be only one fundamental issue: could Britain,
however battered and bowed, permit herself to be internationally humiliated by a junta composed of arrogant,
murderous and absurdly ignorant generals who, peering
myopically towards London, had convinced themselves
that we would not, could not, react.

Bearing in mind our recent history it's perhaps not
surprising that they had come to this conclusion, and,
indeed, there were several moments when I myself felt
doubt, and not a little pessimism, about whether our
government would be prepared to pursue the gamble of
confrontation through to the very end. For no one in the
know in Buenos Aires ever believed there could be a real
compromise. In my opinion, it is eternally to Mrs Thatcher's
credit that she sent the task force and, above all, that she
stuck it out. It was a display of nerve that no snide remarks
about the 'inevitability' of our victory or the government's
failure to predict the crisis, can detract from.

I must confess that, in some senses, my views on this
issue are formed by prejudice: the experience of having
worked as a reporter in Argentina during this crisis. The
word 'fascist' is one I normally hesitate to use — even when
it was coined few people seemed able to define it. But of
all the countries I have visited Argentina comes closest to
any obvious definition of a fascist state. It's not just the
total absence of the democratic process, the untramelled
power wielded by various sections of the armed forces or
the brutal and manipulative methods that a succession of

would-be dictators have used to try to maintain their hold on power. The inhumanity of the Argentine state is most apparent at the level of the individual, who quite simply has no rights—not even, in the end, the right to exist. Secret police forces can only suppress political opposition if, at the last resort, there is no accountability to restrain their behaviour, no way, however tortuous, of making the secret inner state that all societies possess, cough up its secrets. Ever since the Perons Argentinians have lived in a society where if, for whatever reason, an individual crossed the invisible line he could be arbitrarily punished or even, quite simply, disappear. The generals now in power have claimed that all these abuses are in the past. But the truth is that the machinery for control through terror remains intact and may, by the time these words are published, have been brought out again.

In this regard the Argentine action in attempting to take over the islands was entirely in context with their character and history. The 1,800 islanders did not want them—no matter, their views would not count. They might just as well not exist. After all, Argentina is the only country in Latin America without any significant Indian population, a happy state of affairs that was arrived at by the simple expedient of massacring virtually all the surviving Indians in the last century. It is pointless and misleading to give any weight to the fact that few of the islanders were mistreated during the Argentine occupation of the Falklands. Quite apart from the fact that they were at the centre of international attention, no one is suggesting that they would have been butchered. Had the junta succeeded, they would quite simply have been given the choice of being 'in harmony' with Argentine society (one of Juan Peron's favourite expressions), or getting out. As an interest group, an idea entirely foreign to Argentine political tradition, they would have been brushed aside. This is a roundabout way of saying that I do not believe that any British government could have retained, not just any credibility, but any private confidence in itself if it had allowed the islanders to take pot luck at the hands of the Argentine junta, no matter what guarantees had been offered.

The answer that the islanders could have been rehoused elsewhere at a fraction of the cost of sending the task force, though neat, is really not sufficient. In real terms it's almost as unrealistic as the people who recommended dropping television sets instead of bombs on the Vietcong. Nations that try to solve their disputes by buying their enemy off can only, in the end, suffer contempt and ridicule. And what finally made this dispute unnegotiable was the nature of the enemy himself. What honourable solution could possibly have been negotiated with the Galtieri junta? What document could possibly have been agreed that would not in the fulness of time have dishonoured and disgraced the British government that signed it?

It's not my intention to make the Falklands appear, even momentarily, like the war with Hitler, recast and on a more controllable scale. *The Sun* newspaper has done more than enough of that already. Fortunately for us Galtieri was, in the end, more interested in the comfort provided by Glenfiddich than in his bluster about last-ditch resistance. At the same time this mini-war has undoubtedly opened up a whole range of moral questions that few people in this country expected to confront in their lifetimes. As a journalist I am still concerned by the outburst of jingoism that erupted in much of the press, and the cries of 'traitor' that were raised in some quarters against anyone who didn't go along with it. I don't see how our profession can hope to be an independent institution within the society, rather than just a system of entertainment and propaganda, if it discards all pretence to objectivity whenever our interests, as opposed to other peoples', are at stake. In spite of these particular worries, however, I am personally proud of what our armed forces achieved in the Falklands, and I would really like to know from critics of the operation what they would have done instead.

23 June 1982

Laurence Meynell

The Argentine invasion was an act of pure aggression and an obvious breach of international law. Nevertheless it would have been wiser not to send the task force for the following reasons: (a) the expense and difficulty of conducting a campaign 8,000 miles from base; (b) we had insufficient air cover and were bound to lose capital ships; (c) even when (if) we succeed in clearing the invaders out of the islands we will be left with a permanent and insupportable problem on our hands.

In conclusion, therefore, I say that instead of sending the task force we should have registered the strongest possible diplomatic protest and referred the whole matter to the International Court of Justice at the Hague.

They would have done nothing about it, but they would have taken a long time doing it, and we would have been spared a war which we can't afford and which is going to alienate all Latin America from us (and in any case, in the long run we don't want the Falklands!)
3 June 1982

George Mikes

This is a ludicrous but necessary war.

One of our war aims ('the wishes of the islanders must be paramount') is absurd. To involve 80 million people in a war for the sake of 1,800 (i.e. 0.0025%) *is* ludicrous. To say that the wishes of 1,800 decent and likeable sheep farmers should ultimately decide the issue of war and peace and — potentially — the fate of our civilization is ridiculous. It is quite wrong to maintain that numbers do not matter. They do. It makes quite a difference whether — say — the Nazis murdered six Jews or six million Jews. They also matter in another way: if the liberty of 1,800 people warrant a bloody war *of principle* what about the liberty of my former compatriots, the Hungarians? Or the Poles? Or the Ukrainians?

The issue is even more ludicrous because no one really *wants* the Falkland Islands. The British, at the bottom of their hearts and in other circumstances would be quite happy to be relieved of them. In Argentina to desire to possess them is not a rational desire but national hysteria. (I do know irredentist madness from my own Hungarian childhood.) They should not be ready to fight and die for a few rocks and a million sheep. But apparently th~y are.

So we have 80 million people involved in a bloody war for the sake of 1,800 sheep-farmers whose interests—with a little more foresight—could have been safeguarded by other means. And a considerable minority of whom have already expressed their wishes: their paramount wish is to get away from the islands and live somewhere else.

But there is another aspect of the matter and there is a serious principle involved. *That* I support wholeheartedly. Generals always fight the last war and diplomats always solve the last crisis. Had Hitler been stopped after the re-militarisation of the Rhineland, then . . . yes, we certainly would have got rid of Hitler but we would have no idea today what we missed. In any case, as it is fairly widely known, we did not get rid of Hitler and we have learnt a bitter lesson. Dictators must not be allowed to grab other people's territories. Yet, a great deal of ludicrousness invades this aspect of the matter too. Should the Argentine junta win, it is the South American states who will find themselves in the most dire danger. Yet, they are the most vociferous supporters of Argentina, a country most of them fear and detest. A European power must not invade their Continent, they maintain. Should the Argentine junta get away with this act of aggression the *Continent* will still remain theirs but huge chunks will be missing from many of their countries.

What is the solution? Aggression must be stopped. But in addition to this principle a lot more: national honour, flag-waving, slogans, chest-beating etc. have also become of 'paramount' importance. So let us give them free flow for a short while, saving as many lives as we possibly can, but once aggression has been checked and national vanities satisfied, let, I suggest, the *losers* have the Falkland Islands. Written on 5th June, 1982, on the day when the final battle for Port Stanley seemed to be imminent.

Spike Milligan

I am for the Government's response to the Argentine annexation of the Falkland Islands.

I don't know [how the dispute should be resolved], I don't think anybody knows, if anybody says they do know they must be out of their minds on an ego trip. I mean, before the Falklands, what about Ulster? Alas, I fear as in all solutions based upon occupation of land, this was done by spilling blood. It has been so since the beginning of time, and it will be so until the end of time. Utopia only exists in the mind.

All solutions are only temporary. The only way to end wars is to have them.
4 June 1982

Naomi Mitchison

I am totally against the war in the Falklands, whatever courage, techical excellence and self-sacrifice it has called out in the participants. Basically it is a war being waged because a political leader felt herself in danger — partly from her own backbenchers whose response is a century out of date as well, I believe, as being morally wrong — and partly from the fact of three million unemployed. Of course the annexation was also caused by the fears of a political group in the Argentine (to whom we have been selling armaments and much else for many years in spite of protests from 'liberals'). The same pattern appears in the even bloodier war in Lebanon.

We seem to be fighting for a company which is allied with Coalite which has no good reputation among those of us who are interested in the environment. Most Falklanders would probably prefer not to be tenants but to have farms of their own elsewhere; that has not been on offer though it would be vastly cheaper than sending a Navy into the sub-arctic waters.

I would like to see a UN task force in the islands for some years; it would be a nice change from their impossible position next to Lebanon. Then, when tempers were down and both armies back at home, there must be a diplomatic solution of the kind which sensible people in the British Foreign Office have been trying to put across. It would be a good thing if all oil exploration round the islands were to be undertaken under the same auspices and might bring some much needed cash to the UN. None of this seems likely so long as the present government remains in power in this country, but possibly other pressures may arise.
9 June 1982

Patrick Moore

Of course the Government acted correctly. Every effort was made to avoid bloodshed; nobody could have wanted war less than Mrs Thatcher did. But had we held back, we we would have been abandoning our people in the Falklands, which is unthinkable.

The only solution now is to maintain a force there strong enough to make sure that there is no further invasion.

It does seem that the Argentinians made a major mis-calculation. Any Prime Minister except Mrs Thatcher, since the time of Churchill, would have allowed them to get away with it! Had this happened, Gibralter would have been the

next to go—followed, possibly, by the Isle of Wight . . .
2 June 1982

Sheridan Morley

No war anywhere ever made any kind of sense, least of all
an undeclared war caused at least in part by a long series of
Foreign Office blunders. Nobody, at least in Britain, much
wanted the Falklands when they were our unchallenged
property; now that they have been challenged, and the first
of our lives have been lost in their defence, we have had to
create a retrospective moral position. This may be shaky,
but for the sake of the families involved we have got to
learn to live with it. The Falklands will doubtless be retaken
by Britain; when they are, we should turn them into the
first really successful South Atlantic holiday camp and
conference centre and let those who would still go to war
do so on banks of Space Invaders.
15 June 1982

Frank Muir

It was flattering to be invited to contribute to *Authors Take
Sides on the Falklands* but my political views on the Falklands are about as worth reading as General Galtieri's views
on 18th century humorous novels.
16 June 1982

Bill Naughton

It is impossible for those who take sides to judge the
Falklands conflict with what we take to be sanity: not, at

least, whilst the problem is an immediate one. It would seem that we become bereft of reason for a time, on that particular question. Each one can see only his or her point of view — the other becoming shut out. Racial and religious issues appear to bring about a like derangement. I look upon it as a reflex action, and have learnt to try and avoid all argument over such questions, putting it down to a quirk of human nature. On occasion I have later discovered myself to have been in the wrong, and have often been left wondering how good may sometimes emerge from apparent evil.

In my own case this prejudice or aberration has taken a form of unyielding pacifism for as long as I can recall — wedded to a rather hot temper. It has worked well for me personally, although initially it lost me what I took to be a good job as a lorry driver, broke up my home, and set me adrift for some years. I'm not sure it would have resolved national conflicts, but I believe it would not have been worse than the nuclear clashes that appear to lie ahead. I cannot pretend to adopt a rational pose to answer your questions, for I consider the Falklands hostilities to have been near heartless lunacy, which might have been solved diplomatically. The exultations of one group of politicians and the rueful excuses of the other having been paid for by death and destruction, and woeful bereavements of the innocent.

During the warfare I found myself recalling a wayside message which I read on a poster outside a Friends' Meeting House some fifty years ago, on my way to sign on the dole: *A defeated enemy*, it read, *will rise again, but a reconciled one is truly vanquished* (Schiller).
19 June 1982

Peter Nichols

Nearly a thousand men have died and thousands of millions of pounds have been spent to lose and retake a barren sheep-station. What began as farce has finished, for most of my countrymen, as a triumph for the British way, for *The Daily Mail*, for Margaret Thatcher and the spirit of vengeance she so clearly embodies.

The first casualty was truth, the second humour and the third an effective opposition. The leader of the Labour Party appealed for our support on the grounds that no one could accuse him of opposing the government! The word 'gallantry' was bayed from the back benches but the only true courage was shown by those who braved threats of castration to say a word for appeasement and the usual practices of peace. The rest of us hid, realising that the bullies of Britain had seen another bully and acted likewise.

And now there's The World Cup, the royal baby and the international arms sales at Aldershot. And after that? Well, 'Chariots of Fire' must be on somewhere . . .
23 June 1982

Norman Nicholson

I am very suspicious and anxious about the British reaction to the Argentine invasion of the Falklands, feeling that it is motivated by hidden atavistic impulses which are not understood by those in power.
12 June 1982

John Julius Norwich

I am whole-heartedly in favour of our Government's response to the Argentine invasion; not, heaven knows, for the sake of the Falklands themselves—which strike me as being as unpleasant a corner of the earth as one might ever fear to find—but in order to make it clear that the law of the jungle cannot and will not be tolerated.

Having said that, I should also like to put on record that I think it would be ridiculous to attempt to hang on to the islands indefinitely. We must of course do so for a time; the Galtieri gang cannot be allowed to claim, in the long term, that they were even indirectly instrumental in obliging us to loosen our hold. If and when a more moderate or more enlightened government assumes power in Argentina, however, I should be in favour of our making a commitment to hand over the Falkland Islands ten years after that time. This would give the Falklanders plenty of time for resettlement, at our Government's expense.
9 June 1982

Kathleen Nott

I think that the Falklands affair should never have been allowed to develop: but that in the event there was nothing else to do but to throw the Argentinians out. Those are for the moment two fairly settled opinions. Behind them there are a number of doubts. I suspect that the crisis was not entirely due to governmental ineptitude, that there are all sorts of things behind of which we know nothing and about which we are unlikely to be directly and officially informed. I also suspect that it was useful to Mrs Thatcher, personally, in the state of our economy, and, more sinister, as a test of our acceptance of worse wars and a rehearsal of our preparedness. Since we do not know what we are cheering for, I feel that we have anyway no cause to cheer. Talk of national honour and unity is tripe whether talked by the Argentinians or by ourselves. It reflects nothing more general and realistic than the equally widespread but still minority-enthusiasms for the World Cup. The Falklands action is like most of our public experiences and choices, probably the lesser of two evils—immediate ones, that is. But chiefly it highlights the immensely larger evil of our present human development. We have to learn to give up killing one another. And that if anything at all can be learned at the end of a long and almost impossibly difficult road: first, perhaps to agree that we ourselves and our present allies don't sell arms to next week's enemies: then an implemented agreement on nuclear disarmament: finally total disarmament. In short, Kingdom Come.

As for the Falklands, I doubt that anyone, the Government included, can foresee the scope and duration of the consequences; even more I doubt that they will benefit most of us.

21 June 1982

Alun Owen

My answer to your question is not to answer your question. For several years I have been boring my family and friends with my insistence that one day the Falkland Islands would either be quietly handed over to the Argentine by the Foreign Office or the Argentine would annex them.

I was deeply distressed when the annexation took place and negotiations broke down and grew daily more alarmed by the following escalation of the deaths of so many young men.

I think the final solution must be with the United Nation if the United Nations is to retain any real credibility and clout in the world.

15 June 1982

John Papworth

It was an act of hair-brained folly to have sent the British task force to the South Atlantic. If there is any morality being practised in these matters, which appears doubtful, we should have recalled Lincoln's words, that the task of a statesman, 'is to set a good example, not follow a bad one'. The Falklands do not belong to Britain, they do not belong to the Argentine, they belong to the people who live there.

Well, of course. But how do we stop them being invaded?

The question goes to the heart of the problem of war and violence in the twentieth century. We may be sure of one thing, the answer is not to be found in that dangerously futile international quango the UN. The UN is an international league of warmongers and it is as unreasoning to expect it to secure the abolition of war as it is to expect an international league of the Mafia to secure the abolition of crime. In any case if we are naive enough to suppose that any organisation can obtain sufficient military clout to stop any war in any part of the planet without becoming a political dictatorship so horrendous as to make Stalin's Russia look like an arcadian dovecot we have clearly not given two minutes consecutive thought to the problem of the safe disposal of political and military power in the modern world.

The origin of the danger of modern global war arises from political and economic giantism. Our nations are out of control and do not respond to human questions for peace because they are too big to be other than compulsive struggles for power-as-an-end-in-itself. The power may be in money, commerce, politics or militarism but owing to giantism it is power which is the prime goal, not human wellbeing.

Only small societies can ensure that human considerations take precedence over power ones. That is why all the cultural glories of the human race have originated in small, human-scale societies, and that is why to this day whereas all the giant nations are warlike, expansionist and belligerent (as well as being bedevilled by many other problems such as inflation and unemployment), the only countries which are pacific, stable, prosperous, and politically relaxed and tolerant are all small. When did the Scandinavians or the Austrians or the Swiss last attack anyone?

We may be quite sure that the answer to global war will come from a source so unexpected and so seemingly weird as to arouse screams of outrage from the orthodox, even if six months later they will be falling over themselves to claim they had thought of it all along.

The answer to the problem of war in the South Atlantic is for the Argentine (population 25 million) to be divided up into four or five or more independent states, none of which will have the power to make serious war on another or to entertain global territorial ambition.

My own guess is that we had better press on with creating a microcellular global order for peace and human-scale living while there is time and before the giants destroy us. But I have not answered the question. Indeed not, for ultimately it has no answer. If people *want* war no power on earth except a totalitarian one will prevent them from waging it.

But modern global wars do not arise because people want them, but because they cannot prevent them. Wars today are sparked off when the size of nations in relation to others reaches a critical point.

'Critical power,' declares Professor Leopold Kohr, 'is the volume of power that gives a country's leaders reason to believe they cannot be checked by the power available to any antagonist or combination of antagonists. Its accumulation is the cause of war, the inevitable cause of war and the only cause of war.'

Hence the need to divide up the globe into units of five or ten million on the lines of the Scandinavians.

Collectively 'Argentina', with millions of square miles of undeveloped land can *afford* to wax bellicose about a few islands nearly four hundred miles from its shores, but the independent sovereign states of Patagonia, Chubut, Rio Negro, La Pampa, Mendoza and other territories which now make up Argentina would no more dream of attacking the Falklands than Norway would dream of attacking Denmark.

Whatever subject of the natural sciences we survey the same law of life prevails, *growth is always accompanied by*

division, not by unification. Only human arrogance makes us suppose that we can achieve a dynamic stability by pursuing the opposite road—that of unity. In medicine we give a name to growth based on a unity in disregard of function, we call it cancer. Our entire globe is suffering from political and economic cancer. The next stage forward in the human adventure is towards the universal adoption of the human scale: small is not only beautiful, it is now a prerequisite to survival.
16 June 1982

Derek Parker

The Falklands issue is in one sense very simple. Britain 'owns' the islands; the Argentines invaded them. Aggressors who simply walk in and take over someone else's land, subjugating their citizens and imposing foreign rule, cannot be allowed to profit from their violence. To that extent Mrs Thatcher could only react in one way, the Opposition was entirely right to support her, and unless one is prepared to take the view that the 'owning' of any land by any group of human beings is wrong (and there is something to be said for that view), there is no other possible attitude.

But there are difficulties. Geographically, who can doubt that the Falklands 'naturally' belong to Argentina? There may be even the tiniest touch of a moral right involved, looking at the islands' history. There seems little doubt that if some way could have been devised by any of the last three or four Governments, of presenting them to Argentina without too obviously betraying the British settlers, they would long since have gone.

Ah, but then there is South Georgia—neighbouring Antarctica—oil—minerals—*money*. The Government's knuckles whitened around the truncheon. And there is the problem of the present Argentine *régime*. Only yesterday the British Government, and certainly the US Government,

were waggling their haunches at General Galtieri's dirty
little junta in a pantomime of seduction (the very attitude
adopted during the war by the Soviet Government, and for
pretty well the same reasons). The irony of British troops
being expertly killed by Western arms escaped no one; nor
that of treating like a soldier and a gentleman the Argentine
commander of South Georgia, much given, for light
recreation, to tipping nuns out of helicopters and experiment-
ing in the conductivity of electricity by human flesh.

The death of one man is too great a price to pay for any
god-forsaken group of desolate islands, if you are that man's
wife and last saw him leaving your wedding reception,
bravely looking the other way. But no Government has
ever been able to afford to think in those terms. Neither
can weight be given to the argument that the war would
suddenly have become unthinkable when more men died
defending the concept of international law than there were
inhabitants on the islands. Either a principle is worth
defending, or it is not. Reluctantly, one must assent to the
view that if Argentina had been allowed to remain on the
Falklands and establish permanent rule there, there would
very soon have been a similar move elsewhere from a much
larger power. Then the soup would really have begun to
boil. Does anyone really believe the UN could have per-
suaded Galtieri to withdraw? Or that the US, terrified that
any part of South America might blush as much as a light
pink, would have acted?

All war is filthy. Some wars are filthy necessities. Unlike
the Vietnam conflict, the Falklands war was that.

Two final points: it is vital that a proper enquiry should
establish how it was that, apparently ignoring warnings and
signals, Mrs Thatcher's Government dropped us so
spectacularly in the shit from which we eventually emerged
singing 'Rule, Brittania!' (how near the surface idiot jingoism lies). And it is even more vital that at the earliest
opportunity, but not before the re-establishment of
democratic Government in Argentina, discussions should
be reopened about the future of the islands. Because of

Argentine behaviour on and off the Falklands, this is a distasteful prospect. But there will be no peace in the South Atlantic until the question is finally settled; and it can never be settled without some accommodation between us and representatives of those cold, shivering, defeated young conscripts many of whom (we are told) were captured believing that they were entrenched somewhere in the Andes.
17 June 1982

Gilbert Phelps

Sheer schizophrenia. I want to believe that war as a means of solving international disputes and colonialism (both British and Argentine) are alike anachronisms. But as an anti-Fascist I would not wish to see the present Argentine regime in control (or sharing in the control) of any islanders, anywhere. The ideal solution would be some sort of international administration—but there is little evidence to suggest that the United Nations would be capable of organising it fairly or effectively. As the idea of 'ownership' is certainly an anachronism, it seems to me that their future must to a very large extent be in the hands of the islanders themselves, hopefully under some form of international guarantee. I cannot see, if we really believe in the principle of democracy, that the smallness of their numbers has anything to do with it.
14 June 1982

David Plante

I believe that the particulars of a political vision, however deeply moral that vision is thought to be, are incidental to a general moral absolute about war: that there are no just wars, that all wars are wrong.
18 June 1982

Anthony Powell

I continue to think that writers are better occupied getting
on with their writing (a view reinforced by previous
surveys of this kind), rather than making group statements
about random political matters.
29 May 1982

James Purdy

I believe that Britain and Argentina should have settled the
matter of the Falkland Islands peacefully many years ago.
The United States has constantly fostered regimes which
are cruel, tyrannical and genocidal in Latin America, and I
am afraid the events in the Falkland Islands will make co-
operation and understanding between the English-speaking
world and Latin America still more difficult.
18 June 1982

Magnus Pyke

In my lifetime I have seen the dreadful slaughter of World
War I in which a generation of young men was senselessly
exterminated. I have lived through the killing and destruction of World War II and witnessed the uselessness of the
subsequent wars—in Korea, in Vietnam, in Zimbabwe—
that followed. I am, therefore, opposed to the use of war
as a means of settling international disputes. With the back-
ing of the UN, I would have censured the Argentines and
then negotiated the sale of the Falkland Islands to them.
After all, the Russians sold Alaska to a North American
republic in 1867 for $7.2m. An equivalent sum from a
South American republic would be ample to settle the
settlers' claims. But a fleet of battleships—no.
9 June 1982

Kathleen Raine

I am indeed dismayed by the diplomatic incompetence
which allowed the situation in the South Atlantic ever to
develop in the first place. The hasty despatching of a task
force was a mistake; we should have consulted the United
Nations and placed the matter in the hands of a body
created for just such situations. We must go back to them
sooner or later in any case. The price of saving those barren
acres at the price of bloodshed (on both sides) is on the
face of it absurd; but of course one knows that material
interests are involved and not the much publicised 'wishes
of the Falkland Islanders'. The only person who spoke
with humanity and good sense was Mr Benn; to whom in
fact I wrote a letter of support, although I have never voted
Labour in my life. The Social Democrats have been feeble,
Labour has spoken with several voices, and the public
reaction has been swayed by sensationalism and an unlooked-
for upsurge of the worst kind of imperialist jingoism. I am
not proud of my country at this moment, although of
course, things being as they are, a quick recapture of the
islands is to be hoped for in order to end the bloodshed.
28 May 1982

Frederic Raphael

Owing to the accumulated ineptitudes of two great depart-
ments of state, the Prime Minister finds herself in the
position of a woman who can do no wrong. What policy
could never procure, accident has contrived. Each side has
made the Falklands affair a matter of national honour,
though its outcome is clearly more vital for the governments
concerned than for the nations they command. If it is the
case that the islands are sovereign British territory, it is also
clear that London was never unwilling to convey them to
the Argentine. We may be shocked by the rape (and the

dago character of the rapist), but no judge would fail to ironise on the flimsiness of the victim's coverings.

The last time the British were faced with solemn obligations, they abandoned Cyprus to the Turks, without even calling for sanctions, even though London wàs the guarantor of Cypriot independence. To maintain that some universal law against violence is being upheld by the Falklands expedition is therefore humbug. The war establishes only that even civilized governments will, when their own tenure is threatened, not hesitate to retrieve their political fortunes by shedding insignificant blood. With the support of a crass press and a credulous public, the British government emigrated from the complexities of today to the simplicities of the eighteenth century. The Prime Minister, goaded by a parliament impatient with domesticity, has eagerly adopted the slogan 'I am their leader, I must follow them'.

In fact, Mrs Thatcher had the prettiest opportunity of divesting herself of an uneconomic encumbrance by dutiful reliance on the United Nations. It is possible, though unlikely, that patient pomposity, backed by sanctions, might eventually have secured a compromise compatible with the vanities of both sides. At best, therefore, no one would have had to die and a diplomatic solution might have been secured; at worst, the British would have been scandalously divested of something they never much wanted to keep. Nothing whatever, in the actual event, has been proved about the futility of violence or the wickedness of fascism. It has merely been shown yet again that when men have decided to breach the sixth commandment, they signal their resolve by singing hymns.

22 June 1982

Piers Paul Read

Initially I felt that the cost of retaking the Falklands was disproportionate to their value but even as I reached this balanced conclusion images of vengeance — the sinking of Argentine ships — sprang involuntarily into my mind.

I then met a man from Trinidad who said it was essential for those off-shore island states which depended upon Britain for their territorial integrity that the Falklands should be retaken. I was convinced by what he said. Reason and atavism were reconciled. I followed the campaign with horror, fascination and pity for the Argentinians who had fallen victim not just to British cluster bombs but their own Latin temperament.
21 June 1982

Mary Renault

If Argentina had been justified in annexing the Falklands, so would France be in seizing the Channel Islands, regardless of any wish expressed by the inhabitants. Do you really think the issue morally controversial? You surprise me.
16 June 1982

Paul Roche

Only three solutions seemed to me possible. One was to do what we did: spend billions, lose lives, and retake the islands by force. The supposed virtue of this was to show the world that England still abides by principle and will stand up to bullies. Its chief defect is that the expense of keeping guard over the less than two thousand people who live there will go on indefinitely.

Another solution would have been to leave the invading Argentinians in possession and give each Falkland house-holder one million pounds compensation, with the choice of staying or coming to Britain. The merit of such a solution would have been that the war was avoided, the future assured, the cost minimal, and a new example given to humanity of how even barefaced robbery can be sublimated and the aggrandisement of gangsters made to look foolish. Perhaps its only disadvantage would have been the loss of six hundred thousand sheep.

My third solution would have been to hand over the islands to Spain (who has the only other possible legal claim), with the proviso that she stopped fussing over Gibralter.

I would overwhelmingly have opted for the second solution.
18 June 1982

Alan Ross

I regard the Government's response as perfectly reasonable, in the initial context.

As things turned out there was no sensible way of resolving the situation other than the means chosen.

This is not to say that things should ever have been allowed to reach a point where the sending of the task force was necessary.

But faced with Argentine intransigence in refusing to withdraw troops it would have been folly to turn back half-way. Some good comes out of a professional job well done, in circumstances more altruistic than is usually the case.

Needless to say, the whole concept of settling disputes by war remains a grotesque anachronism.
8 June 1982

Salman Rushdie

I am against the British Government's response to the Argentine landings on the Falklands for three reasons:

because it was hypocritical; because it effectively committed Britain to war before a peaceful settlement could be negotiated; and because of the xenophobic militarism it unleashed here in Britain.

Hypocrisy first. We were told the Argentines were to be hated because they were a fascist regime. This did not prevent us from selling them arms until March of this year. It does not prevent us from being allies, within NATO, of the fascist government of Turkey. It does not prevent us from maintaining close trading links with, or from selling arms to, South Africa. It has not, in the recent past, prevented British governments from supporting the fascist Shah of Iran; but there is no point in continuing the list. It seems that the only bad fascists are the ones who turn our own weapons against us. (I use the word 'us' as a naturalized British subject; but I use it more uneasily than ever before. I have never felt more alien from Britain than I do now.)

The British government has always been expert at tailoring its moralizing to its interest. When Uganda-based British citizens were in danger, 'we' defended their right not to live under fascism by passing laws to keep them out of Britain. But they, of course, were black.

This war was fought to drown the noise of our own diplomatic chickens coming home to roost. It was a war to save Mrs Thatcher's face, which may, in time, become as notorious as Jenkins's ear. It is not a face worth launching a thousand ships, or even a task force, to rescue.

Now for my second objection. UN resolution 502 did not merely call for an Argentine withdrawal, although that was the part the British government stressed. It also called for the conflict not to be escalated by either side. After 502, every act of escalation was committed by the British. It's impossible not to believe that Mrs Thatcher wanted a war from the beginning. She sneered at the UN before the war began; now, ungenerous in peace, she sees no role for the UN in this affair. Hers are the politics of the Victorian nursery; if somebody pinches you, you take their trousers down and thrash them. The terrible, ironic effect of her

policy has been that a war which we were told was fought
to prove that aggression did not pay has ended up proving
the exact opposite. The world's armies are already queueing
up for Harrier jump-jets and Exocet missiles.

We live in the nuclear age; and the Falklands War has
shown us how, one day, a nuclear war, that most final of
solutions, might begin. It will begin because the language
and logic of the pre-nuclear period are still in use. I believe
it to be vital that 'we' abandon this language and logic;
because any war may turn into the last war, no war is worth
starting any more, ever. As a nuclear power, Britain has it
in her power to end history. This places upon her leaders a
responsibility they show no signs of being willing to face.

The huge support given by the British people to this war
doesn't need much discussion. I wish only to say that it
has made me feel ashamed.

Your second question—about the manner in which the
dispute should be resolved—has been a little overtaken by
events. But at some point in the future, some British government will wish to desist from maintaining a huge and
expensive garrison on the Falklands. Before the war, we had
been trying for years to find a 'solution' to the Falklands
problem (i.e. a way of handing the islands over to Argentina).
The war does not alter the absurdity of retaining them; it
only intensifies it, because after all the deaths and sunken
ships the Kelpers have not been given back what they lost.
They have been given an army camp.

Whenever this sinks in, negotiations with Argentina
(which is not going to float away across the ocean) will have
to be resumed. The UN has been enfeebled precisely because
the Thatchers of our age are all too ready to leave its conference rooms to hurl their lethal toys at one another. We
shall have to hope that when we decide to talk, the proper
forum for the conversation is still in being. Because of
course the only proper way to proceed is to talk. Careful
talk saves lives.

22 June 1982

Vernon Scannell

I am entirely opposed to our Government's response to the
Argentine annexation of the Falklands and I believe that it
would have been possible to arrive at a settlement by
negotiation through the offices of the United Nations. Mrs
Thatcher's reaction to the news of the invasion was un-
surprising, but that the Leader of the Opposition should
join her stentorian supporters and commit his party to a
more or less unqualified approval of their imprudent and
aggressive jingoism shocked me deeply. The question that
everyone who approves Britain's exercise of armed strength
in the South Atlantic should ask himself, or herself, is this:
'Would *I* be prepared to be killed or horribly maimed in
order that the Falkland Islands should retain British
Sovereignty?' My own answer to that question is a loud
and unequivocal 'No!' and I cannot help wondering if
some of those ferocious Tory back-benchers would be so
eager for a military solution if it were they who would have
to run the risk of being burned to death or blown to pieces.

First, then, I object to the British 'solution' on the
grounds that an alternative means could with patience,
intelligence and imagination, have been found and no lives
need have been lost. Next, because at a time when unemployment and its miserable consequences are pestilential
in our society, when education, health and other vital
welfare services are being eroded because, as the Prime
Minister has repeatedly said, 'we have not the money',
billions are being wasted in the prosecution of this fruitless
and unnecessary adventure. And finally because I believe
that the British Public is being duped by its leaders whose
ineptitude caused the crisis by which they have, incredible
though it may seem, won unprecedented popularity.

At the time of writing the British land forces are preparing for the last stage in the campaign to capture Port
Stanley. It seems that this action will inevitably involve
heavy casualties on both sides; more bloodshed, agony and
death. No surrender terms have been offered to the enemy

garrison. The total defeat and humiliation of the Argentinians is the goal of the British Government and it is one
which, if and when it is achieved, will be followed by
disastrous national and international consequences. And
when the whole grim episode is completed and tidied away
into the pages of history it will not be seen as a time of
glory, as *The Sun* newspaper and too many of our politicians
would now have us see it, but as a disgraceful, stupid and
squalid consequence of mismanagement, pride and
selfishness.

Postscript: It occurs to me that the foregoing comments
might seem like a blanket condemnation of war in any
circumstances, an expression of absolute pacifism. I should
just like to add that, though I am in favour of unilateral
disarmament, I am not and never have been a total pacifist.
I served in the infantry in World War II and saw action in
the Middle East and in Normandy where I was wounded. I
believe that in certain circumstances the use of military
force can be justified and that the war against the Axis
powers was one such instance. But I am equally convinced
that the present action in the South Atlantic is totally
unjustified.

2 June 1982

Martin Seymour-Smith

I am against the Government's response to the Argentine
annexation of the Falkland Islands.

Mrs Thatcher was dealing with thugs, and knew the
situation. In 1977 a similar situation was defused without
even reaching the newspapers. Three ministers have resigned,
and, as the person who sees all the telegrams and ought to
know what is going on, she should go, too. But she won't
because politics is a dishonourable business, and getting
more so.

The task force was sent too soon, or not slowed up

enough *en route*, as it could have been. Had the advice of
the Air Chiefs been taken then we should have had better
air-cover, and lives would have been saved.

There is little excuse for the heavy destruction suffered
by our ships. There must have been some bungling, since
defence against the weapons the Argentines used is possible.
One can only assume that Mrs Thatcher and her advisors
were in a tearing hurry to 'make Britain great again'.

A government's demeanour is a part of its response. Mrs
Thatcher's speech denouncing a perfectly balanced Panorama
programme (which I watched), was, quite simply, a denun-
ciation of the right to free speech. No questions of security
were involved (though one of the officers slaughtered was
going to sue the BBC World Service for the information it
gave the Argentines—about which Mrs Thatcher has,
apparently, no comment). Further, no criticism was made
by anyone in the Government of the attitude taken up by
the gutter press, which rejoiced in the slaughter of the
Argentines in an unequivocal manner. Now we know what
Mrs Thatcher really feels about the concept of 'democracy'
which she uses so often.

'Violence must not be seen to succeed.' True. But
violence has been done to thousands more than the 1,800
who live on the Falkland Islands: in the torture chambers
of the governments of Chile, El Salvador—and of course
Argentina. When has Mrs Thatcher objected to this? Indeed,
when she denounces communist governments and communist aggression, she seldom if ever refers to their
violations of individual rights (such as use of force against
the person). She is clearly not interested in this aspect of
tyranny of the right, or alleged left—only of the fact that
the unfairly rich might have some of their money taken
from them.

We have been trying to get rid of the Falklands for years,
though no doubt the 'enquiry' will absolve us of this. We
have made no attempt to understand in what way the
Argentine people (victims of a series of gangsters) feel about
the islands. But a civil servant did write in 1936 that our

act of piracy in taking them made our case for holding
them that much harder. Mrs Thatcher would gladly have
sold out the Falklanders had things gone in another way,
just as she has sold out the NHS and all else she hates. (I
should add that I do not consider her to be a Tory, and that
I find the behaviour of the opposition parties, with a few
honourable exceptions, as bad as hers.)

The South Atlantic dispute ought to be settled by a UN
occupying force. It is rightly said that the UN 'have no
teeth'. But then what government has ever really wanted it
to have teeth? They could be given real power if governments
wanted this.

That this squalid affair, relieved only by the gallantry of
our forces and the skill of their commanders, has made
Britain 'great again' is a notion that can only make a decent
person feel sick. That is what the men who took part in
the operation seem to feel.

The imagination of Mrs Thatcher fails at so elementary
a point that it is frightening. This was said to me by a life-
long Tory. This affair and her demeanour throughout, not
to say her blunders, have demonstrated this beyond doubt.
She is the worst prime minister of the past two centuries,
and perhaps the most insensitive of all time; this affair has
made it clear that the responsible members of her party
should remove her.

22 June 1982

Alan Sillitoe

I think that by the time this reply gets printed the Falkland
Islands will be back where they belong—under British
administration. For my part, I certainly hope so. Last
October I spent some days in Toronto, attending a conference run by Amnesty International and the Toronto
Committee of Human Rights, and what I heard there
about the horrific atrocities committed by the Argentine

regime against its own people came back to me on hearing of the occupation of the Falkland Islands. There is no reason to suppose that the British residents of those islands would fare any better than the Argentines. I was therefore wholeheartedly in favour of the islands being recovered as soon as possible, by overwhelming and irreversible military force if necessary.

I find it sad that socialists seem always to be united in their antagonism to military resistance against a fascist act, with the consequence that the situation invariably gets worse. In the streets of London certain so-called socialists actually carried banners indicating support for the Argentine Junta, which should of course, considering the history of the 20th century, surprise nobody.

Neither do I believe that the Argentine has any legal claim to the Falkland Islands. They are several hundred miles from the nearest point on the mainland. When the British recover them they should keep their sovereignty as long as it is militarily possible to do so. A proper airbase should be established, and any commercial links which had connected the islands to Argentina before the invasion should not be reopened.

11 June 1982

Muriel Spark

In reply to your question, I am in favour of our response to the Argentinian annexation of the Falkland Islands.

You also ask how I think the dispute in the South Atlantic should be resolved. I think it should be resolved according to the wishes of the inhabitants of the Falkland Islands.

8 June 1982

Paul Theroux

It seems to me laughable that a hundred desk-bound book-worms should offer opinions on a military campaign that we know about only from what we have read in newspapers we usually sneer at. Can anyone honestly say that he knows what is going on in the South Atlantic? And as of today — 7 June — the war is not yet over.

Speaking generally, all disputes ought to be settled by negotiation rather than murder. Surely this is obvious? War is sometimes necessary, but it is only thrilling to the onlooker who is watching from a safe distance. In fact, it is disgusting, frightening, cruel, reckless, inhumane and overpriced.

How interesting that in this Falklands business each side believes that God is supporting her, and has rustled up an archbishop to say so. God, I am glad I'm an alien.

D.M. Thomas

Most of the people in the world live under tyrannies: many, like the Soviet Union or Poland, claiming to be democracies; others, marginally less odious, like Argentina, having the honesty to admit that they have no popular mandate. We who are privileged to live in true democracies are generally helpless to assist the enslaved people. When Argentina took over the Falkland Islanders by naked force we were, for once, not helpless. We committed ourselves to restoring freedom; if possible by negotiation, by force if necessary. I supported that commitment, and continue to do so. The *junta* is responsible for the tragic loss of life.

Had we not sent the task force, or failed to use it when the *junta* rejected ultra-generous withdrawal terms, the islanders could have said goodbye to their freedom or their homeland. Left to the United Nations, the 'minor' act of aggression would have been consigned within weeks to the trashcan of history, superseded by greater conflicts. The only honest alternative to the British government's action was to admit frankly that the islands were gone and it was just rough luck on their inhabitants. That, in my view, would have been shameful. Those who oppose our use of force have often quoted *Hamlet*: 'We go to gain a little patch of ground / That hath in it no profit but the name.' (IV, iv). There has been fashionable sneering at the barrenness and remoteness of the islands, as though such 'deficiencies' should somehow reconcile the kelpers to settling elsewhere, as though a wilderness cannot be loved as dearly as a paradise. Hamlet himself, in fact, did not share the scepticism of Fortinbras's Captain. He reflects: ' . . . Rightly to be great / Is not to stir without great argument, / But greatly to find quarrel in a straw / When honour's at the stake.' Honour, in the present conflict, means not jingoistic vainglory but a determination to uphold freedom and self-determination.

Just as the Falklands conflict has been the last 19th century war, so one would hope that the problem might eventually find a 21st century solution: that the islands might become international territory, with international guarantees of the islanders' freedoms.
7 June 1982

Hugh Thomas

My views on the Falklands are these: the invasion by Argentina on April 2 was a deliberate act of aggression. It was condemned by the UN in its Resolution 502. After that, the Argentines went on to commit other acts of aggression, in South Georgia.

Britain had, therefore, to respond. If we had turned 'the other cheek', we should have cast doubt on our whole credibility in relation to other possible threats. Also we could not have abandoned the Falklanders. How could we have imagined handing them over to the tender mercies of the Junta? Had we done so we should have helped the cause of military dictators throughout Latin America.

We were of course right to negotiate to begin with, even though some of the concessions made in late April or early May might have been hard to accept, since they would have seemed to have given some kind of prize to the Junta.

In the end, the British action was exemplary and I supported it with all my heart.
13 June 1982

Polly Toynbee

The government stumbled blindly into war, and after the first taste of blood, discovered the joys of singing Rule Brittania to the accompaniment of rising opinion polls. It is bloody, pointless and lacking in any reasonable objective for a long term solution.

What should we do? Mrs Thatcher has closed her options. Our options are open. Remove her from office, withdraw our troops, and negotiate to hand over sovereignty to the Argentine with reasonable guarantees to the Falklanders. We should give the islanders the choice of removal with generous compensation paid for by the Argentine. All we have to lose is national pride, and politicians' faces. Those things are not worth fighting for. Very little ever is.
7 June 1982

Keith Waterhouse

I supported our response—but not its supporters, baying for blood and toasting 'Our Boys' in gin-and-tonic. Patriotism may not be enough but jingoism is too much.
18 June 1982

Auberon Waugh

In its historical context I cannot see Britain's defence of the Falkland Islands as anything but an absurdity, however valiant.
1 June 1982

Arnold Wesker

1. Underlying most conflicts, and the preparedness to die for them, is the acceptance that concepts about the *way* life should be lived are more important than life itself. But I believe there is only one concept more important than life, and that is the concept which embodies a belief that life is more important than concepts. Sacrifice may be asked for that. In the Falklands conflict I see Argentina defending a concept about the *way* the lives of 1,800 Falklanders should be lived, and the UK as defending life itself.
2. With the facts known to me it is difficult to understand how the Falklands dispute was allowed to continue for so long or how the UK government was unable to read the signs of invasion.
3. My contempt is divided between those in our country who allowed the situation to reach this extreme point, and the murderously stupid Argentine military leaders who believed bullying force would achieve their ends.
4. No government which sells arms to fascist or totalitarian states can then be morally righteous about the state's aggressive actions.
5. No state whose own history is rooted in colonialism can be righteous about analogous histories. I cannot see that a difference can be made between a 500-year-old right—the majority of the population of Argentina is of European descent, and a 150-year-old right—which is the length of time the British descendents have lived on the Falklands.

With Brecht I would say:

> What there is shall belong to
> those who are good for it, namely
> the children to the motherly ones
> the cars to the good drivers
> and the valley to the irrigators
> so that it may bear fruit.

6. I despise and mistrust the motives of Generals who have no sense of the absurdity of their pomposity, who grab power and assume the control of the lives of civil populations, and who in old age seek last minute glory in war. No country should be run by the military.

7. I sense in the world a growing attachment to primitive emotionalism. The invasion of the Falklands reflects this.

8. Reports of the abuse of human rights by the Argentine authorities are horrifying. 1,800 islanders could not possibly survive under them.

9. The Task force had to be sent. It should have led to a peaceful withdrawal under UN supervision of Argentinian forces who could have declared they had achieved their objective both of focusing world attention on their claims and of putting the British to enormous expense as the price of their dilatoriness. The UK made many genuine concessions during the UN negotiations including that they would in good time be prepared to surrender sovereignty. The Argentine negotiators seemed devoid of the natural or diplomatic wisdom to enable them to read between the lines.

10. I'm driven to the desperate and uncomfortable conclusion that depressing and tragic though it is for the price paid, the task force have no alternative but to fight on until occupying Argentine forces surrender.

28 May 1982

Patrick White

I played a very minor role in the World War II which
ended at Hiroshima and Nagasaki. From what I saw for
myself in the London Blitz and the Western Desert and
Libya, and what I have heard tell of the horrors of Japan, I
am against war of any kind: conventional weapons are
lethal enough and can lead to worse. As for the Falklands
dispute, I see the Argentine Junta as the worst kind of
Fascist regime, but Thatcher and her tribe, and the unspeakable President Reagan, seem to me no better. I shall
do everything in my power to discourage Australian youth
and the youth of anywhere else from becoming involved in
the futilities of war. We must continue talking to one
another in the human language we have in common, and
avoid letting ourselves be rushed into false patriotism by
ambitious or desperate politicians, armaments manufacturers,
and scientists whose job it is to supply their political bosses
with a bigger and better means of destruction.
10 June 1982

Heathcote Williams

This war, like all wars—from the Anglo-Saxon *wirra* which
means 'confusion'—has the whiff of bestiality with a dodo.
18 June 1982

Stop Press!

The following pieces arrived too late for inclusion in the
main body of the book and the authors are not in
Appendix 1

Paul Ableman

I am both for, and against, the Government's response to
the Argentine occupation of the Falklands. I am for it as a
patriotic Englishman proud of the spirit of democracy which
is so deeply-rooted in these islands and of the Government's
determination to preserve the liberties of British subjects
everywhere. The cause was a just one. I am against the
Government's response because, as the Pope said, the age of
warfare is over. Any war could now escalate into a nuclear
confrontation which could exterminate life on the planet.
The negative view is incomparably the weightier.

How should the Government have responded? In a world
of sovereign states ultimately dependent on force for the
promotion of their real or imagined interests, there was no
other way it could have brought about the desired end: the
removal of the Argentine forces. The fault lies with a world
composed of independently armed nations. Since an
increasing number of these nations are armed with nuclear
weapons the result is suicidal anarchy. The truth is that
there is *no* correct way that governments, as governments,
can behave in a planet that now has a global civil and
military technology. The need is for an effective supra-
national authority and ultimately a world government.
National governments are naturally the greatest impediment
to the establishment of such an authority since it would
necessitate their dissolution. National governments have
therefore become at best an irrelevancy and at worst a
hindrance in the quest to eliminate war and ensure human
survival. A massive global popular movement is the only
hope.
4 July 1982

Dannie Abse

The pure, pale criminal is one who admits to killing his
victim solely because he enjoys the dramatic act of murder.

For no other reason. Does he exist outside the pages of
fiction? A real nice human-type murderer wishes to be
thought of as sane, if not by others, then by himself. So in
a gloomy cell he whispers to the Father Confessor or to the
psychiatrist what he thinks to be the true cause of why he
dismembered so bloodily his victim. The reason given may
be momentous or apparently trivial: Because, Father, the
swine was possessed by the devil, because, doctor, the
swine stole my wife; because, Father, the swine had
treasure under the floorboards; because, doctor, each night
the swine came into my garden and ate my gooseberries.

We who go to war, to patriotic murder, need for sanity's
sake a cause. The Greeks besieged Troy because beautiful
Helen, they sincerely believed, had been abducted, forced
into a coloured ship that sailed for Troy. Yet there is
another legend, another report, less sensational: Helen never
went to Troy. She left home, yes, but not for Troy and
she was not forced. She was elsewhere, Egypt perhaps,
Cyprus perhaps, and those Trojans, those Greeks, slaughtered
each other for ten long years because of a fairy story, a
lying headline, a cloud, a ghost, an empty garment. I am one
who believes this other story, that Helen was spotted by
travellers on the banks of a delta:

> Deep girdled, the sun in her hair, with that way of standing...
> The lively skin, the eyes and great eyelids,
> She was there, on the banks of a Delta.
>   And at Troy?
> Nothing. At Troy a phantom.
> So the gods willed it.
> And Paris lay with a shadow as though it were solid flesh:
> And we were slaughtered for Helen ten long years.

We British are an aggressive nation. We seem to have
become more violent this last decade: look how we drive
fast and furious, with fists clenched; listen, at the stadiums,
how the crowds shout, 'Kick his fuckin' head in,' or to the
sirens of police-cars and ambulances in the shoddy streets of
Brixton or Liverpool. Listen to the usual thud of an explosion

in Belfast. Most of the time, though, we turn our aggression
inwards, we punish ourselves: we elect a leader who believes
in Capital Punishment, who can punish us with conviction
and with style, who with her male, public-school educated
legions can sanguinely dismantle our Health Service, ruin
our cities, pollute the air with lead or radioactivity, and
make us unemployed.

Once we were told, You've never had it so good, and
indeed we had never had it so good. It seems we felt we
did not deserve it; our left hand was guilty; and our right
hand was so guilty that we needed relief, we needed to be
punished. But, mother and margaret, six of the best was
not enough, is still not enough. We still have aggression to
spare. We boil over. Ulster is getting boring; besides, there,
the issues are not black and white, they're complicated,
confused. What we need is a clear issue. If we are going to
murder anybody, God, we must have a clear issue, we must
be *virtuous*. So what about a faraway island, one most of
us have never heard of before — oh don't tell us about
treasure offshore — if we murder it must be for a pure
principle.

No question, the Argentinian government are thugs in
uniform. Yes, Argentinian thugs, who can deny that? It is
true, it is documented. What a cause! What a Helen! So pass
the drum, the gun and the blood-drip. Ta ra ra. Ta ra ra.
Ta ra ra.
9 July 1982

Kingsley Amis

1. For.
2. Those who answered 'For' to Question 1 have in doing
so answered Question 2 as well, but Woolf and Wilson are
so touchingly sure of an 'Against' answer that they take no
account of that. Given its purpose, Question 2 is naturally
full of equivocation. To call the Falklands business a
'dispute' is to prejudge it as a mere difference of opinion

between two much-of-a-muchness factions. And the question itself is really two questions, one about ends, one about means, but that doesn't matter to the right kind of respondent, whose answers to both of them have got the necessary something to do with our side giving in.
24 June 1982

Thomas Balogh

I find your proposed assembly of 'views' quite interesting. There are great snags.

(i) Why should *authors as such* know about the twists and complexities of political action.

(ii) We shall not know until the enquiry's report is published what actually happened.

(iii) Subject to (i) and (ii) I think that the Government neglected the danger of invasion and of the long run impossibility of insisting that the Falklands should remain Crown Colonies.

(iv) In view of this (iii) the Government ought to have passed the responsibility to the United Nations.

(v) After the invasion of the Falklands by Argentina a military response was inevitable but the Government ought to announce that they would consider a conference (U.N., U.S.A., Argentina, Brazil, others (?)) and try to bring about an international regime for the Falklands.

(vi) A refusal by us to do this would increase the burden of defence to impossible levels and might lead to a painful loss of foreign trade.
30 June 1982

Melvyn Bragg

My overwhelming feeling throughout was irritation that we (i.e. Thatcher's Government) could have been so stupid as to have let it happen. There was also the embarrassment of of realising how contrary this sudden Little Falklander attitude was to our recent policy which was clearly moving towards letting them drift off to the South American mainland. Finally, hopelessness that such an insignificant, relatively straightforward conflict of interests could not be resolved without recourse to war.

Or did 'we' really want and need a war? Do we and will we increasingly deliberately seek out 'insignificant' issues in order to spend the desire for war comparatively safely? The Falklands could be an indicator of future 'engagements'.

All that said, however, the Argentines behaved illegally: neither the USA nor the UN were going to get them off the Falklands. We had to do *something*. The task force ought to have alerted Galtieri to the grimness of the possibilities he had uncorked. Unfortunately he was too foolish and too boxed in to react in any other than a hostile manner.

I supported the intention to take back the islands: I supported the British Forces' difficult job. We had got ourselves into a mess where there was no obviously honourable cause. We fudged things with unnecessary expense of life. I cannot believe that 'doing nothing' would, in the short or long term have been preferable. Someone had to redress the wrong.

The dispute ought to be resolved by our admitting that sovereignty can, ultimately, be negotiated. Unhappily, the war and the understandable fears of the Falkland islanders will put back by many years the date at which that can become acceptable.

Apart from everything else, the Falklands' issue raised some of the worst aspects of the British character: armchair gloating, bombastic boasts, incompetence and recriminations, and in miniature, most of the casualties of war.

8 July 1982

Raymond Briggs

If the Falkland Islands are so important to the British, it would be interesting to know why the Falkland Islanders

lost their British nationality under the 1981 Nationality
Bill; why they have no M.P.; why they are not entitled to
a British pension; why they get all their major education in
Argentina; and also, if the Argentine regime is so bad, how
is it that several thousand British people have chosen to
live there? If the regime is so corrupt why have the British,
for years, been selling them arms and training their servicemen?

Surely, economic pressure (if only the denial of armaments, training and spares!) by the USA and the EEC
combined must have forced Argentina to negotiate.

This issue was not worth the sacrifice of one single life.

Now there is the irony that the Argentines did not harm
a single Falklander, but three have died, all killed by the
British.

2 July 1982

André Brink

Each act of violence — and all the more so if it is the act,
not of an individual but of a nation or a government —
represents a defeat of human progress and a regression to
an earlier stage of evolution. Humanity itself is its victim;
there are no victors.

23 June 1982

Elizabeth Jennings

Clearly, no foreign power has the right to invade another.
So, we *had* to do something about the Argentinians enter-
ing the Falklands. However, as Lord Carrington was deeply
engaged in Middle East troubles *and* might have prevented
what has happened there now, the blame cannot be fairly
laid on him and, in fact, *no-one* has blamed him for anything. There are facts now which reveal that we *had*
received threats of this invasion, so many that, very

understandably, we thought they *were* mere threats. At a
terrible price of heroic courage shown in all our Services, we
overthrew the Argentinians. *But* a bitter lesson has been
learnt i.e. that we should have a large and totally modern
Navy. I hope the present Government will make this a
high priority.
30 June 1982

Colin MacCabe

I am against the Thatcher Government's response to the
Argentine invasion of the Falkland Islands.

History is not important in this affair; geography and
the wishes of the islanders are. Geography makes it clear
that the Falklands are Argentinian. The wish of the people
is clearly to stay British. The obvious solution is to grant
Argentina sovereignty over the islands but delay any
Argentinian administration, or indeed any presence on the
islands (other than their flag) until it became clear that
the islanders would be willing to accept Argentinian administration. This might take over 50 years, over 100 years.
The period would certainly be shortened when Britain
stopped supporting a foreign policy which encourages the
establishment of brutal military dictatorships in Third
World client states.

It is totally unclear that the solution proposed above
(the 'lease-back' solution) was ever seriously proposed
before the invasion or, more importantly, after the task
force set sail. If it had been proposed seriously after the
invasion then Thatcher would certainly have fallen victim
to the Tory right but thousands of others would not have
fallen victim to the Western armaments industry.
9 July 1982

Derwent May

Everyone must regret the loss of life in the Falklands. But
a nation which sincerely believes that democracy and

individual freedom are its proper goals could not have let
the Argentinians stay on the Falklands without the
complete loss of its self-respect. Moral arguments about
respecting the Argentinians' sense of honour were either
hypocritical or hopelessly muddled: to defer to a cruel,
Fascist sense of honour in preference to standing up for
one's own decent sense of honour was a morally indefensible
position. Equally, arguments from Realpolitik — 'we mustn't
upset South America' — have already proved false, not to say
cowardly: everyone we respect in America, North or South,
has been glad to see the junta defeated.

After the fighting, it is impossible to envisage any acceptance of Argentinian claims to the Falklands in the near
future. The Falklanders themselves may take a different
view in the distant future, and then the situation can be
reconsidered. Meanwhile, we must look to those countries
who share our ideals to help us maintain peace and security
there — or else shoulder the burden alone, as the only course
compatible, again, with our self-respect.

4 July 1982

Ivor Montague

The first question, alas, is a loaded one. There has been no
Argentine 'annexation' of the Falkland Islands. The only
annexation concerned is that of the Malvinas by Britain
which took place in the 19th century.

Granted the strength of nationalist feeling over such
matters nowadays, and the precarious position as well as
atrocious nature of the two governments concerned, the
resort to force by the one was always on the cards and the
arrogant response by force of the other, having been
caught napping, inevitable.

The problem is not how should the dispute be resolved
but how can it be. The only way in which it ever will be
resolved is by extension of the agreed international co-
operation in the Antarctic hitherto carried out in

exemplary fashion by those participating, not against each other, but side by side.

As was to be expected in this case the military violence has only made matters worse. In this particular area there is no intrinsic reason of interest preventing improvement and safeguards for the islanders with a mutually negotiable special role for both Britain and Argentina, and every reason making this desirable in view of the past historical concern of both. But the stubbornness and stupidity of those involved on either side, reinforced by the wounds of conflict and exacerbated by the humbuggery and malice usual in such situations, constitutes even if the sole, nevertheless a currently invincible, obstacle. After all, it had never been a habit of Mrs Thatcher to listen to good advice.

However, no other solution can possibly be lasting. The important task will be to bear patiently this target in mind, to encourage the development of more sensible and less atrocious and suicidal governments on both sides, and meanwhile to ensure that no actions on the part of either, or on that of any of the hyenas lurking around, are allowed to be used to empoison the promising present pattern of Antarctic co-operation, a precious, if still limited, model to the world.

17 June 1982

Jan Morris

I believe the Falkland Islands war to have been unnecessary in origin, distasteful in execution, tragic in outcome and unproductive in consequence.

I think the dispute should have been solved by a transfer of sovereignty to the Argentinians, supported by United Nations supervision of the islands' administration, and financial help to those islanders who would prefer to emigrate.

But I may be wrong.

30 June 1982

Robert Nye

1. For. 2. As it was.

22 June 1982

Roland Penrose

The UN were right to condemn an act of aggression when
the Argentine junta took by force South Georgia and the
Falkland Islands but those British colonies had already
become an anachronism, relics of the British sea power
which is now merged into NATO.

The indignation shown by a Tory government was that
of a poacher become game-keeper. In its new rôle, if it is
sincere, support for UN discussions is comprehensible but
if international law is to be upheld as the 'raison d'être' of
this conception, the UN must be given the power to
enforce it. When they hoisted the Union Jack again at
Port Stanley the UN flag should have been raised beside it.
Otherwise the British call for its support is seriously tainted
with hypocrisy.

5 July 1982

Tom Pickard

The Admiral said 'I'm just a commuter from Surberton.'
ASLEF beware.

There seems to be a bottomless purse and an unlimited
number of young lives available to defend 1,800 disen-
franchised white wool gatherers who dump more than
35,000 carcasses per year in pursuit of their career on a
god-forsaken island eight thousand miles from here — while
at home our freedom-loving government is introducing a
bill which will make it very difficult for citizens here to
defend themselves properly in court unless they happen to
be wealthy. The action this government took in the South

Atlantic was fanatical and shameful. There was no justification for the loss of life and the maiming of young bodies on either side. The Argentinian action provided Britain, which is a vastly superior military power, with a golden opportunity to show some faith in the United Nations, however long it took to resolve the problem. Even if that failed it would still not justify the loss of a single life. Better to furnish the islanders with a decent way of life elsewhere. But wasn't it jolly lucky we won the war in time for the Arms Sales at Aldershot? I hope you get a nice bonus Maggie (paid to party funds of course). Submit this to MoD before publication and ask for clearance.

5 July 1982

John Rae

Machiavelli is the only authentic guide. There is no place for morality or sentiment in foreign policy. The only yardstick for judging the Government's response to the Argentine annexation of the Falkland Islands is Britain's interests. I have no doubt that the Government's response was correct. It cannot be in a nation's interests to allow its sovereign territory to be seized with impunity by a foreign power. It makes no difference whatsoever that the Argentine Government is a military dictatorship. We should have responded in the same way if Galtieri had been the Archangel Gabriel.

In trying to find a resolution to the dispute in the South Atlantic we must again be guided by our national interests. If the islands have some economic or strategic importance to us we should hang on to them. If they do not, we should make it clear to the islanders that we cannot protect them indefinitely and that it is in their interests as well as ours to negotiate with the Argentines about the islands long term future.

26 June 1982

George Wigg

I was opposed, and remain opposed, to the Government's response to the Argentinian annexation of the Falkland Islands.

I accept that public opinion, stimulated by an illiterate media, made it increasingly difficult for Mrs Thatcher to follow the dictates of common sense and submit Britain's case to the International Courts of Justice, and express immediately and without reservation our country's willingness to accept the judgement of that Court.

I believe it to be of fundamental importance that nations should act within the framework of international law—for resort to force is not only barbaric, it is an offence against reason and in the long run self-defeating. The only foundation upon which the peace of the world can be established and maintained is within the framework of universal acceptance of international law.

28 June 1982

Arthur Hailey

Of course Britain was right and honorable in restoring self-determination to the people of the Falklands. I find it inconceivable that any intelligent, thoughtful person with an awareness of history can argue otherwise.

The Falklands represented a precedent. If the latter-day Argentine nazis had been allowed to succeed with their unprovoked aggression against an unwilling populace, nowhere in the world would have been safe from similar invasions any more.

It has often been said that 'Hitler could have been stopped at the Rhine'. I believe it equally true that Britain's courage and adherence to moral principle during the Falklands crisis showed plainly that a willingness to fight for freedom still exists. Moreover, the deserved defeat and humiliation of the Argentine dictators may well have delayed World War III for a decade and perhaps far longer.

The free world, especially the United States, owes a tremendous debt to Britain and the Thatcher Government. How Afghanistans must wish that they were a part of the British Commonwealth too!

14 July 1982

The Contributors

JOAN AIKEN (b. 1924): English novelist and writer of children's books. *Night Birds on Nantucket* (1966); *A Touch of Chill* (stories) (1980); *The Lightning Tree* (1980).

BRIAN ALDISS (b. 1925): British science fiction writer, novelist, poet, playwright, critic and editor. *Perilous Planets* (1978); *New Arrivals, Old Encounters* (1979); *This World and Nearer Ones* (1979); *Pile* (verse)(1979); *Life in the West* (1980).

JOHN ARDEN (b. 1930): British playwright and director. *All Fall Down* (1955); *Serjeant Musgrave's Dance* (1959); *Soldier, Soldier* (1960); *Armstrong's Last Goodnight* (1964); *Soldier, Soldier and Other Plays* (1967); *The Soldier's Tale* (1968); *To Present the Pretence* (essays)(1978); *Pearl* (1978).

A.J. AYER (b. 1910): English philosopher. *Language, Truth and Logic* (1936, 1946); *The Foundations of Empirical Knowledge* (1940); *Logical Positivism* (1959); *Perception and Identity* (1979). Wykeham Professor of Logic at Oxford.

C.J. BARTLETT (b. 1931): English biographer and historian, specialising in international history. *Great Britain and Sea Power, 1815-53* (1963); *Castlereagh* (1966); *The Long Retreat: A Short History of British Defence Policy, 1945-70* (1972); *The Rise and Fall of the Pax Americana* (1974); *A History of Postwar Britain, 1945-1974* (1977). Professor of International History at Dundee.

MAX BELOFF (b. 1913): English historian and writer on politics and international affairs. *The Foreign Policy of Soviet Russia* (1947, 1949); *Thomas Jefferson and American Democracy* (1948); *Europe and the Europeans* (1957); *The Great Powers* (1959); *The Balance of Power* (1968); *The Intellectual in Politics and Other Essays* (1970); co-author *The Government of the United Kingdom* (1979). Created Life Peer, 1981.

MICHAEL BOGDANOV (b. 1938): British dramatist and an associate director of National Theatre since 1980. Co-author of plays, adaptations and children's theatre pieces.

VINCENT BROME: English novelist and biographer. *H.G. Wells* (1951); *The Way Back* (1957); *The Problem of Progress* (1963); *Love in Our Time* (1964); *The International Brigades* (1965); *Freud and his Early Circle* (1967); *G.G. Jung* (1978); *Havelock Ellis* (1979).

BRIGID BROPHY (b. 1929): English novelist, dramatist and literary critic. *Hackenfeller's Ape* (1953); *The Finishing Touch* (1963); *The Adventures of God in His Search for the Black Girl* (1973); *Palace Without Chairs* (1978).

ALAN BROWNJOHN (b. 1931): English poet, writer of children's books and literary critic. Also writes as John Berrington.

Travellers Alone (1954); *The Lion's Mouth* (1967); Selected
Poems in *Penguin Modern Poets*, vol. 14 (1969); *Brownjohn's
Beasts* (1970); *A Song of a Good Life* (1975); *Philip Larkin*
(1975).

PETER CADOGAN (b. 1921): British political writer. General
Secretary, South Place Ethical Society since 1970. Founding
Secretary, East Anglian Committee of 100, 1961. Secretary,
National Committee of 100, 1965-68. *Extra-Parliamentary
Democracy* (1968); *Direct Democracy* (1974; rev. edn 1975);
Early Radical Newspapers (1975); *Six Ballads for the Seventies*
(1976).

JAMES CAMERON (b. 1911): Scottish author, journalist and
foreign correspondent. *A Touch of the Sun* (1950); *Mandarin
Red* (1955); *The African Revolution* (1961); *The Making of
Israel* (1977).

JILLY COOPER (b. 1937): English novelist, children's writer and
columnist (*The Sunday Times* and *The Mail on Sunday*). *How to
Survive from 9 to 5* (1970); *Women and Superwomen* (1974); *Super
Jilly* (1977); *Imogen* (1978); *Supercooper* (1980); *The British in
Love* (1980); *Little Mabel's Great Escape* (1981).

ROALD DAHL (b. 1916): English short story writer, writer of
children's books, screenwriter, playwright and novelist. *The
Gremlins* (1943); *Someone Like You* (1953); *James and the Giant
Peach* (1961); *Charlie and the Chocolate Factory* (1964); *Fantastic
Mr Fox* (1970); *Charlie and the Great Glass Elevator* (1972);
Danny the Champion of the World (1975); *My Uncle Oswald*
(1979).

TAM DALYELL (b. 1932): author and weekly columnist, *New
Scientist*, since 1967. *The Case of Ship-Schools* (1960); *Ship-
School Dunera* (1963); *Devolution: the End of Britain?* (1977);
One Man's Falklands . . . (forthcoming, 1982). Scottish MP (Lab.)
West Lothian since 1962; Opposition Spokesman on Science from
1980 until sacked by Michael Foot on the Falklands issue in 1982;
Parliamentary Private Secretary to Richard Crossman, 1964-70;
Chairman of Parliamentary Labour Party Foreign Affairs Group,
1974-76.

WILLIAM DOUGLAS-HOME (b. 1912): Scottish playwright, poet
and autobiographer. *Home Truths* (poetry, 1939); *The Chiltern
Hundreds* (1947); *The Reluctant Débutante* (1955); *The Colditz
Story* (screenplay, 1957); *The Bishop and the Actress* (1968);
Lloyd George Knew My Father (1972); *Mr Home Pronounced
Hume: An Autobiography* (1979).

MARGARET DRABBLE (b. 1939): English novelist, playwright and
biographer. *A Summer Bird-Cage* (1963); *The Garrick Year* (1964);
The Millstone (1965); *Jerusalem the Golden* (1967); *The Waterfall*
(1969); *The Needle's Eye* (1972); *Arnold Bennett* (1974); *The
Realms of Gold* (1975); *The Ice Age* (1977); *The Middle Ground*
(1980).

RICHARD EBERHART (b. 1904): American poet, playwright and literary critic. Ed., with S. Rodman, *War and the Poet* (1945); *Collected Verse Plays* (1962); *Selected Poems, 1930-65* (1965); *Collected Poems, 1930-76* (1976); *Ways of Light* (1980).

H.J. EYSENCK (b. 1916): English writer on psychology and psychotherapy. *Dimensions of Personality* (1947); *The Structure of Human Personality* (1952); *The Dynamics of Anxiety and Hysteria* (1957); *Crime and Personality* (1964); *The Inequality of Man* (1973); *The Structure and Measurement of Intelligence* (1979). Professor of Psychology in the University of London, and Director of the Psychological Department at the Institute of Psychiatry (Maudsley and Bethlem Royal Hospitals).

IAN FLETCHER (b. 1920): English poet, playwright, literary critic and biographer. *Orisons, Picaresque and Metaphysical* (poetry, 1947); *Partheneia Sacra* (1950); *The Complete Poems of Lionel Johnson* (1953); *Walter Pater* (1959, rev. edn 1972); *Beaumont and Fletcher* (1967); *Swinburne* (1973); ed., *Decadence and the 1890s* (1979).

PETER FRYER (b. 1927): English author. *Hungarian Tragedy* (1956); *Mrs Grundy* (1963); *The Birth Controllers* (1965); *Private Case—Public Scandal* (1966); *The Road to Brixton: a History of Blacks in Britain* (due for publication by Pluto, 1983).

RAYMOND GARLICK (b. 1926): Welsh poet and critic. *Collected Poems, 1954-68* (1968); *An Introduction to Anglo-Welsh Literature* (1970, 1972); *A Sense of Time* (1972); *Incense* (1976).

DAVID GASCOYNE (b. 1916): English poet, playwright, novelist and literary critic. *Poems, 1937-42* (1943); *Thomas Carlyle* (1952); *Collected Poems* (1965); *The Sun at Midnight* (1970); *3 Poems* (1976); *Paris Journal, 1937-39* (1978).

STELLA GIBBONS (b. 1902): English novelist, humorist and poet. *Cold Comfort Farm* (1932); *Christmas at Cold Comfort Farm and Other Stories* (1940); *Collected Poems* (1951); *The Woods in Winter* (1970).

PENELOPE GILLIATT: English short story writer, novelist, film critic and film scriptwriter. *One by One* (1965); *What's It Like Out? and Other Stories* (1968); *Sunday Bloody Sunday* (screenplay, 1971); *The Cutting Edge* (1978); *Three-Quarter Face* (1980); two one-act plays produced in New York in 1980; *But When All's Said and Done* (play, 1982); *The Beach of Aurora* (full-length opera libretto, 1983).

RUMER GODDEN (b. 1907): British novelist, poet, short story writer and writer of children's books. *Chinese Puzzle* (1936); *Fugue in Time* (1945); *Kingfishers Catch Fire* (1953); *The Kitchen Madonna* (1967); *Mr McFadden's Hallowe'en* (1975); *Five for Sorrow, Ten for Joy* (1979).

CHRISTOPHER HAMPTON (b. 1946): English playwright. *When Did You Last See My Mother?* (1966); *Total Eclipse* (1968); *The Philanthropist* (1970); *Savages* (1973); *Treats* (1976); *Socialism in a Crippled World* (1981); *Pelican Radical Reader* (1983).

TIM HEALD (b. 1944): British mystery novelist and biographer. *It's a Dog's Life* (1971); *Deadline* (1975); *Let Sleeping Dogs Die* (1976); *John Steed: An Authorized Biography* (1977).

PATRICIA HIGHSMITH (b. 1921): American novelist, specialising in crime, and short story writer. *Strangers on the Train* (1950); *A Game for the Living* (1958); *The Tremor of Forgery* (1969); *The Snail-Watcher and Other Stories* (1970); *Edith's Diary* (1977); *Slowly, Slowly in the Wind* (stories, 1979).

CHRISTOPHER HILL (b. 1912): English historian. *The English Revolution, 1640* (1940); *Lenin and the Russian Revolution* (1947); *Intellectual Origins of the English Revolution* (1965); *Change and Continuity in Seventeenth Century England* (1975); *Milton and the English Revolution* (1978); *Some Intellectual Consequences of the English Revolution* (1980). Master of Balliol College, Oxford, 1965-78; Visiting Professor Open University, 1978-80.

BEVIS HILLIER (b. 1940): English writer on art and journalist. *Pottery and Porcelain, 1700-1914* (1968); *Art Deco of the 1920s and 1930s* (1968); *Posters* (1969); *Cartoons and Caricatures* (1970); *The New Antique* (1977).

DAVID HOLBROOK (b. 1923): English poet, novelist, critic and educational writer. *English for Maturity* (1961); *The Secret Places* (1964); *Flesh Wounds* (1966); *Object Relations* (1967); Selected Poems in *Penguin Modern Poets*, vol. 4 ((1963); *Education, Education, Nihilism and Survival* (1977); *Moments in Italy* (1978).

MICHAEL HOLROYD (b. 1935): English biographer, critic and novelist. *Hugh Kingsmill* (1964); *Lytton Strachey* (1967-68); *Augustus John* (1974-75); *The Genius of Shaw* (1979).

MICHAEL HOROVITZ (n. 1935): English poet and translator, editor and publisher of *New Departures* since 1959. *Alan Davie* (1963); *Strangers* (1965); *Poetry for the People* (1966); *Bank Holiday* (1967); *Love Poems* (1971); *Growing Up: Selected Poems and Pictures, 1953-78* (1979).

MICHAEL HOWARD (b. 1922): English historian, specialising in military history. *Disengagement in Europe* (1958); *The Franco-Prussian War* (1961); *Studies in War and Peace* (1970); *War in European History* (1976); *War and the Liberal Conscience* (1978). Professor of History, Oriel College, Oxford.

P.J. KAVANAGH (b. 1931): British poet, novelist, television playwright and autobiographer. *One and One: Poems* (1959); *On the Way to the Depot*; *A Song and a Dance* (novel, 1968); *Edward Thomas in Heaven* (verse, 1974); *People and Weather* (novel, 1978); *Life Before Death* (verse, 1979); *The Irish Captain* (novel, 1979).

LUDOVIC KENNEDY (b. 1919): British writer on current affairs and historian. Television and radio journalist since 1955. *Sub-Lieutenant* (1942); *Nelson's Band of Brothers* (1951); *Murder Story: The Trial of Stephen Ward* (1964); *The Portland Spy Case* (1978); *Meran* (1979).

FRANCIS KING (b. 1923): English novelist, poet, writer of short stories and critic. *To the Dark Tower* (1946); *The Dividing Stream* (1951); *The Last of the Pleasure Gardens* (1965); *The Needle* (1975); *Christopher Isherwood* (1976); *The Action* (1978).

JAMES KIRKUP (b. 1923): British poet, playwright, writer on travel and of non-fiction for children, literary critic, autobiographer and translator. *The Drowned Sailor and Other Poems* (1947); *The Spring Journey and Other Poems of 1952-53* (1954); *The Love of Others* (novel, 1962); *The Refusal to Conform: Last and First Poems* (1963); *White Shadows, Black Shadows: Poems of Peace and War* (1970); *Steps to the Temple* (1979). Professor of English, Japan's Woman's University, Tokyo, since 1963.

G. R. WILSON KNIGHT (b. 1897): English literary critic, poet, playwright, biographer and autobiographer. *The Wheel of Fire* (1930); *The Burning Oracle* (1939); *Christ and Nietzsche* (1948); *The Last of the Incas* (play, 1954); *The Golden Labyrinth* (1962); *Gold Dust* (poetry, 1968); *Neglected Powers* (1971); *Shakespeare's Dramatic Challenge* (1977); *Symbol of Man* (1978). Professor of English Literature, Leeds University, 1956-62.

MARGHANITA LASKI (b. 1915): English novelist and critic. *Little Boy Lost* (1949); *The Victorian Chaise-Longue* (1953); *Ecstasy* (1961); *Jane Austen and Her World* (1969); *George Eliot and Her World* (1973); *Everyday Ecstasy* (1980).

PETER LEVI (b. 1931): English poet and translator and writer on travel. *The Gravel Ponds* (1960); *Water, Rock and Sand* (1962); co-translator of *Yevtushenko: Selected Poems* (1962); *Fresh Water, Sea Water* (1965); *Life is a Platform* (1971); Selected Poems in *Penguin Modern Poets*, vol. 22 (1973); *Five Ages* (1978).

JACK LINDSAY (b. 1900): Australian historian, biographer, novelist and writer on art. Has written 76 works of fiction, plays, story collections, volumes of verse, and books on history, art and autobiography from 1923-59. Recent works: *The Monster City: Defoe's London, 1688-1730* (1978); *The Writing on the Wall: The Crisis in Marxism* (1981).

DAVID LODGE (b. 1935): English novelist, critic and editor. *Ginger You're Barmy* (1962); *The British Museum is Falling Down* (1965); *Language of Fiction* (1966); *Graham Greene* (1966); *How Far Can You Go?* (1980).

NORAH LOFTS (b. 1904): English novelist, mystery writer and biographer. Also writes as Peter Curtis and Juliet Astley. *Dead March in Three Keys* (1940); *The Little Wax Doll* (1970); *Queens of Britain* (1977); *Emma Hamilton* (1978); *Ann Boleyn* (1979).

ETHEL MANNIN (b. 1900): English novelist, short story writer, biographer and writer on travel and child education. *Confessions and Impressions* (1929); *Privileged Spectator* (1939); *Late Have I Loved Thee* (1948); *Rebels' Ride* (1964); *Young in the Twenties* (1971); *Sunset Over Dartmoor* (1977).

JULIAN MANYON (b. 1950): British reporter and television journalist with Thames TV. *The Fall of Saigon* (1976). Covered the Falklands crisis from Buenos Aires, where he was kidnapped by Secret Police and later interviewed General Galtieri.

LAURENCE MEYNELL (b. 1899): English mystery writer, novelist and children's writer. *Smokey Joe*; *Hookey Goes to Blazes*; *The Great Cup Tie* (1974).

GEORGE MIKES (b. 1912): Hungarian-born humorist and publicist, resident in England since 1938. *How to be an Alien* (1946) and the 'How to' series; *The Hungarian Revolution* (1957); *Not by Sun Alone* (1967); *The Prophet Motive* (1969); *The Spy Who Died of Boredom* (1973); *English Humour for Beginners* (1980).

SPIKE MILLIGAN (b. 1918): Irish humorist, poet, playwright and children's writer. *The Bed Sitting Room* (co-author of this play with J. Antrobus); *Oblomov* (play); *Son of Oblomov* (play); *A Book of Goblins* (verse, 1978); *Open Heart University* (verse, 1979).

NAOMI MITCHISON (b. 1897): Scottish novelist and children's writer. *The Conquered* (1923); *The Corn King and the Spring Queen* (1931); *Memoirs of a Spacewoman* (1962); *The Cleansing of the Knife* (poetry, 1979); *Images of Africa* (1980).

PATRICK MOORE (b. 1923): English writer on astronomy and children's writer. *Planet Mars* (1950); *Out into Space* (1954); *The Solar System* (1958); *The Sun* (1968); *The A to Z of Astronomy* (1978); *The Sky at Night* (vol. 6, 1978); *Your Book of Astronomy* (1979).

SHERIDAN MORLEY (b. 1941): British drama critic, scriptwriter, biographer and television journalist. *A Talent to Amuse: the Life of Noel Coward* (1969); *Review Copies* (1975); *Oscar Wilde* (1976); *Sybil Thorndike* (1977); *Gertrude Lawrence* (1981).

FRANK MUIR (b. 1920): British humorist and writer on social history. *The Frank Muir Book* (1976); *What a Mess* (1977); *Take My Word for It* (with Denis Norden, 1978).

BILL NAUGHTON (b. 1910): British novelist, short story writer, children's writer and playwright. *A Roof Over Your Head* (1945); *One Small Boy* (1957); *Alfie* (play, 1963, novel 1966); *Spring and Port Wine* (1965); *The Bees Have Stopped Working and Other Stories* (1976); *My Pal Spadger* (1977).

PETER NICHOLS (b. 1927): British dramatist. *A Day in the Life of Joe Egg* (1967, screenplay 1972); *The National Health* (1969, screenplay 1972); *Forget-me-not Lane* (1971); *Privates on Parade* (1977).

NORMAN NICHOLSON (b. 1914): British poet, playwright, novelist and writer on the Lake District. *Five Rivers* (1944); *The Fire of the Lord* (novel, 1946); *The Old Man of the Mountains* (play, 1945); *William Cowper* (1951); *Provincial Pleasure* (1959); *No Star on the Way Back*; *Ballads and Carols* (1967); *Stitch and Stone* (1975); *The Shadow on Black Combe* (1978).

JOHN JULIUS NORWICH, 2nd Viscount (b. 1929): English historian, travel writer, writer of historical documentaries for television, and literary critic. *The Normans in the South* (1967); *Sahara* (1968); *The Kingdom in the Sun* (1970); *A History of Venice* (2 vols, 1977, 1981).

KATHLEEN NOTT: British novelist, poet and philosophical critic. *Mile End* (1938); *Poems from the North* (1956); *A Clean Well-Lighted Place* (1960); *The Good Want Power: An Essay in the Psychological Possibilities of Liberalism* (1977).

ALUN OWEN (b. 1926): British dramatist. *Progress to the Park* (1958); *Maggie May* (1964); *Shelter* (1967); *The Male of the Species* (1969); *There's Shelter* (1967).

JOHN PAPWORTH (b. 1921): British writer on economics and politics. Anglican clergyman. *Economic Aspects of the Humanist Revolution of Our Time*; *New Politics* (1982). Founder and for several years editor of *Resurgence*. For nine years he worked as Personal Assistant to President of Zambia, Dr Kenneth Kaunda.

DEREK PARKER (b. 1932): British poet, writer on radio, literature, psychology, travel, dance and astrology, and biographer. *The Fall of Phaeton* (1954); *Byron and His World* (1968); *Astrology in the Modern World* (1970); *John Donne and His World* (1974); *Radio: the Great Years* (1976); *The West Country and the Coast* (1980).

GILBERT PHELPS (b. 1915): English literary critic, novelist and playwright. *A Man in his Prime* (1955); *The Russian Novel in English Fiction* (1956); *Deliberate Adventure* (radio play, 1968); *Latin America* (1970); editor: *Wanderings in South America* etc. by Charles Waterton (1973); *Tragedy of Paraguay* (1975).

DAVID PLANTE (b. 1940): American novelist and translator. *The Ghost of Henry James* (1970); *Slides* (1971); *Relatives* (1972); *Figures in Bright Air* (1976); *The Family* (1978); *The Woods* (1980).

ANTHONY POWELL (b. 1905): English novelist, critic and autobiographer. *Afternoon Men* (1931); *What's Become of Waring?* (1939); *John Aubrey and His Friends* (1948); 12 volumes of 'The Music of Time' sequence (1951-75); *Infants of the Spring* (autobiog., 1976); *Messengers of Day* (autobiog., 1978); *Faces in My Time* (autobiog., 1980).

JAMES PURDY (b. 1923): American novelist, playwright and poet. *63: Dream Palace* (1956); *Malcolm* (1959); *Mr Evening: a Story and Nine Poems* (1968); *The Running Sun* (poetry, 1971); *In a Shallow Grave* (1976); *Narrow Rooms* (1978); *Lessons and Complaints* (poems, 1978); *Two Plays* (1979).

MAGNUS PYKE (b. 1908): British writer on nutrition and television journalist. *Manual of Nutrition* (1945); *Nothing Like Science* (1957); *Food, Science and Technology* (1964); *Technological Eating* (1972); *Six Lives of Pyke* (1981).

KATHLEEN RAINE (b. 1908): English poet and literary critic. *Collected Poems* (1956); *Blake and Tradition* (1968); *The Oracle in the Heart: Poems, 1974-78* (1979); *The Inner Journey of the Poet* (1982).

FREDERIC RAPHAEL (b. 1931): American novelist, playwright

and screenwriter. Lives in England and France. *The Limits of Love* (1960); *Lindmann* (1963); *Like Men Betrayed* (1971); *Heaven and Earth* (1983).

PIERS PAUL READ (b. 1941): British novelist, playwright and writer of documentaries. *The Junkers* (1968); *Monk Dawson* (1970); *The House on Highbury Hill* (television play, 1972); *The Story of the Andes Survivors* (1974); *The Train Robbers* (1978); *A Married Man* (1979).

MARY RENAULT (b. 1905): English-born novelist, historical novelist and writer of non-fiction for children; has lived in South Africa since 1948. *The Friendly Young Ladies* (1944); *North Face* (1948); *The Last of the Wine* (1956); *The King Must Die* (1958); *The Bull from the Sea* (1962); *Fire from Heaven* (1970); *The Praise Singer* (1978).

PAUL ROCHE (b. India, 1928): English poet, playwright, novelist and translator. *O Pale Galilean* (novel, 1954); *The Rank Obstinacy of Things: A Selection of Poems* (1962); *To Tell the Truth: Poems* (1967); *The Kiss* (1975); *With Duncan Grant in Southern Turkey* (1981).

ALAN ROSS (b. 1922): English poet, writer of children's fiction and on cricket and travel. *Poetry 1945-50* (1951); *Something of the Sea: Poems 1942-52* (1954); *Australia 63* (cricket; 1963); *North from Sicily: Poems in Italy 1961-4* (1965); *Living in London* (1974); *Open Sea* (1975); *Notes on Death Valley* (1979).

SALMAN RUSHDIE (b. 1947): Indian-born British novelist. *Grimus* (1975); *Midnight's Children* (winner of the Booker Prize, 1981).

VERNON SCANNELL (b. 1922): English poet, novelist, literary critic and autobiographer. *The Masks of Love* (Heinemann Award for Poetry, 1960); *Edward Thomas* (1962); *Selected Poems* (1971); *The Tiger and the Rose: An Autobiography* (1971); *A Proper Gentleman* (1977).

MARTIN SEYMOUR-SMITH (b. 1928): British poet, literary critic, biographer and writer on sexology. *All Devils Fading* (1954); *Fallen Women* (1969); *Reminiscences of Norma: Poems 1963-70* (1971); *Sex and Society* (1975); *Fifty European Novels* (1979); *Robert Graves* (1982).

ALAN SILLITOE (b. 1928): English novelist, short story writer, poet, playwright, screenwriter and writer of children's books. *Saturday Night and Sunday Morning* (1958; screenplay 1960); *The Loneliness of the Long Distance Runner* (1959, screenplay 1961); *The Rats and Other Poems* (1960); *The Death of William Posters* (1965); *A Start in Life* (1971); *Snow on the North Side of Lucifer* (poetry, 1979); *The Storyteller* (1979).

MURIEL SPARK: British novelist, poet, playwright, literary critic and writer of short stories and children's books; lives in Italy. *The Comforters* (1957); *Memento Mori* (1959); *The Ballad of Peckham Rye* (1960); *The Bachelors* (1960); *The Prime of Miss Jean Brodie* (1962); *The Girls of Slender Means* (1963); *The*

Mandelbaum Gate (1965); *Collected Poems I* (1967); *Collected Stories I* (1967); *The Abbess of Crewe* (1974); *Territorial Rights* (1979); *Loitering with Intent* (1981).

PAUL THEROUX (b. 1941): American novelist, short story writer, poet and critic; lives in England. *The Great Railway Bazaar* (1975); *Picture Palace* (1978); *The Old Patagonian Express* (1979); *World's End* (1980).

D.M. THOMAS (b. 1935): English poet and novelist. *The Flute-Player* (Gollancz Pan/Picador Fantasy Award winner, 1979); *Dreaming in Bronze* (poetry, 1981); *The White Hotel* (1981).

HUGH THOMAS (b. 1931): British historian, novelist and biographer. *The Spanish Civil War* (1961, 1977); *The Suez Affair* (1967); *Cuba: or the Pursuit of Freedom* (1971); *John Strachey* (1973); *An Unfinished History of the World* (1980). Chairman, Centre for Policy Studies since 1979; Professor of History at the University of Reading, 1965-75.

POLLY TOYNBEE (b. 1946): English novelist and journalist. *Leftovers* (1966); *A Working Life* (1970); *Hospital* (1977).

KEITH WATERHOUSE (b. 1929): British novelist, dramatist and writer on social history and humour. *There is a Happy Land* (1957); *Billy Liar* (1959; play with Willis Hall, 1960; screenplay, 1963); *A Kind of Loving* (with W. Hall, 1962); *Whoops-a-Daisy* (1968); *Lock Up Your Daughters* (with W. Hall, 1969); *Office Life* (1979); *Rhubarb, Rhubard* (1979).

AUBERON WAUGH (b. 1939): English novelist and columnist: *Private Eye* since 1970; *The Spectator* since 1976; Chief Book Reviewer, *Daily Mail*, since 1981. Novels: *The Foxglove Saga* (1960); *A Path of Dalliance* (1963); *Who Are the Violets Now?* (1965); *Consider the Lilies* (1968); *A Bed of Flowers* (1972).

ARNOLD WESKER (b. 1932): English playwright. *Chicken Soup with Barley* (1959); *Roots* (1959); *I'm Talking About Jerusalem* (1960); *The Kitchen* (1961); *Chips With Everything* (1963); *Their Very Own and Golden City* (1964); *The Four Seasons* (1965); *The Friends* (1970); *The Journalists* (1975); *Collected Plays and Stories* (5 vols., 1980); *Caritas* (1981).

PATRICK WHITE (b. 1912): Australian novelist, playwright and poet; born in London and brought up partly in England, partly in Australia; lives in Australia. *Happy Valley* (1939); *The Tree of Man* (1955); *Voss* (1957; winner of 1st annual literary award from W.H. Smith & Son, 1959); *Riders in the Chariot* (1961); *The Solid Mandala* (1966); *The Cockatoos: Shorter Novels and Stories* (1974); *The Twyborn Affair* (1979). Awarded the Nobel Prize for Literature in 1973.

HEATHCOTE WILLIAMS (b. 1941): British dramatist. Associate editor, *Transatlantic Review*; founding editor, *Suck*. *The Speakers* (1964; adapted as a play, 1974); *The Local Stigmatic* (1965); *Malatesta* (screenplay 1969); *AC/DC* (1970); *Hancock's Last Half-Hour* (1977); *Severe Joy* (1978).

Chronological Summary
of the Background

1592   Englishman, John Davis, claims to have sighted the
            Falkland Islands from his ship, *Desire*. (Argentine
            historians argue that either Ferdinand Magellan or
            Amerigo Vespucci discovered the Falklands.)
1594   Sir Richard Hawkins sails along the islands' north coast.
1598   Dutchman, Sebaldus van Weerdt visits the islands and
            names them the Sebald Islands.
1690   Another Englishman, John Strong, sails between the two
            main islands, lands on one of them and calls the passage
            Falkland Sound. This is the first known landing.
early 1700s Breton sailors from St Malo first to settle on the islands
1722   French map names the islands *Isles Malouines*. (This later
            becomes the Spanish *Islas Malvinas*.)
1764   French establish the first official settlement at Port
            Louis, 20 miles north-west of the present capital, Port
            Stanley, on East Falkland.
1767   France sells East Falkland settlement to Spain for
            £25,000.
1765   Meantime Commodore Byron (grandfather of the poet)
            takes possession, on behalf of England, of the small West
            Falkland island of Saunders, on the grounds of prior
            discovery. The English and Spanish settlers remain in
            ignorance, real or allegedly, of each others' presence until
            1769/70 when Byron's action brings England and Spain
            close to war.
1770   Spanish expel British from West Falkland.
1771   Spain yields West Falkland to Great Britain by con-
            vention, but within 3 years the government in London
            order Governor Clayton to evacuate the islands with his
            garrison.
            The Spanish stay on in East Falkland at Puerto de
            Soledad but by 1811, with Argentina's fight for
            independence, Spain takes no further interest in the
            islands. Argentina afterwards claims that Spain's title has
            passed automatically to Argentina.
1820   Government in Buenos Aires sends ship and claims the
            then unoccupied Falklands for the newly independent
            Republic.
1824   Louis Vernet, a Hamburg merchant of French descent,
            granted right by Buenos Aires to make settlement on East
            Falkland. Buenos Aires appoints a 'Commandant of the
            Malvinas'.

1828/9	Vernet, despite British protests, obtains the title of military and political Governor from the Argentines, i.e. 'sovereignty' of East Falkland.
1831	As a result of a dispute over fishing rights, the Americans send USS *Lexington* to Puerto de la Soledad, to arrest Argentines, spike the guns, destroy armaments and declare the islands free from all government.
1831/2	Argentines appoint new Governor, Juan Mestivier. But Mestivier is murdered shortly after arrival as a result of a mutiny.
1832	Britain despatches sloop *Clio* to the islands. Takes West Falkland in December.
1833	*Clio* arrives at East Falkland on New Year's day to reassert British sovereignty there too.
1834	British Governor is installed and the islands remain under unbroken British rule until 2 April 1982

────────────────────1965────────────────────

1965	UN General Assembly resolution calling for Anglo-Argentine talks about the Falklands.
1966	Armed commando of right-wing Peronist Argentines seize Port Stanley but eventually surrender.
Sept. 1967	Labour Foreign Secretary, George Brown, starts talks with Argentine Foreign Minister on the sovereignty of the islands. Britain prepared to forego sovereignty if assured that the islanders' rights and way of life can be preserved.
early 1968	Beginning of a campaign by a group of Conservative MPs to 'keep the islands British'.
Nov. 1968	Lord Chalfont fails to persuade the islanders of advantages of an agreement with Argentina.
Dec. 1968	Conservative spokesman on Foreign Affairs, Sir Alec Douglas Home, declares that if a Conservative government is returned it will 'strike sovereignty from the agenda'.
1970	Conservative government *is* returned under Edward Heath which *does* 'strike sovereignty from the agenda'.
1971	Argentina agrees temporarily to shelve their claim to sovereignty while they try to win the islanders over.
1973	Perónist government returns to power in Argentina and Argentine claims to sovereignty immediately renewed in UN.
late 1973	Governor of islands requests Royal Navy frigate to be sent, but is refused.
1977	Small group of Argentine sailors put ashore on British island of Morrell, South Sandwich Islands. Argentines claim this is for purposes of scientific research. British government, under James Callaghan, launches a new peace initiative, with question of sovereignty open to negotiation again.

Oct. 1977   Argentina starts preparing for naval 'manoeuvres', which alarm the British.

Nov. 1977   Callaghan sends two frigates and a nuclear submarine to the South Atlantic and Argentine naval 'activities' subside.

Nov. 1980   Conservative Minister of State (in Mrs Thatcher's government), Nicholas Ridley, suggests a 'lease-back' agreement to the islanders, which fails.

late 1981   Conservative government announce that HMS *Endurance* is to be withdrawn from the islands. British Antarctic Survey announce that budgetary cuts will mean closing their base at Grytviken on neighbouring island of South Georgia.

————————————1982————————————

2 Feb.   In a private letter to a Tory party activist the Prime Minister makes clear that she regards the presence of 75 Royal Marines in Port Stanley as sufficient to prevent an Argentine invasion.

25 Feb.   Conservative Foreign Office Minister, Richard Luce, flies to New York for more talks with the Argentines, who suggest establishment of a negotiating commission, to meet monthly and to attempt to reach a conclusion by the end of 1982. (Argentina wants the islands back by 1983, the 150th anniversary of British rule there.)

18 March   Scrap metal merchant, Constantine Davidoff, encouraged by Argentines to land illegally at Leith on British island of South Georgia with about 40 men.

26 March   SIS source in Buenos Aires warns that an Argentine invasion of Falklands is imminent, but government dismisses warning. Argentine navy set out on scheduled manoeuvres with Uruguayan fleet.

28 March   Foreign Office minister, Richard Luce, begins to fear an invasion.

29 March   Joint Intelligence Committee reports to Britain that an invasion seems imminent.

2 April   Argentines arrive in Port Stanley and raise the Argentine flag.
             Emergency Cabinet meeting at 10 Downing Street.

Sat. 3 April House of Commons meets in an emergency session and is told that the task force is to be sent.
             Lord Carrington resigns.
             The Security Council of UN passes Resolution 502, ordering cessation of all hostilities, withdrawal of all Argentine troops from the islands and calling upon Britain and Argentina to seek a diplomatic solution to their differences and fully to respect the purposes abd principles of the UN Charter.

7 April   Britain declares 200-mile war zone around Falklands.

9 April	American Secretary of State, Alexander Haig, undertakes mediation.
10 April	EEC, excluding Italy and Ireland, backs trade sanctions against Argentina.
17 April	Alexander Haig talks with Argentine military junta.
19 April	Haig negotiations break down. Peruvian initiative follows.
25 April	Royal Marines recapture South Georgia.
30 April	President Reagan publicly declares support for Britain.
2 May	Argentine cruiser *General Belgrano* sunk by British submarine outside war zone.
5 May	Peru drafts peace plan.
7 May	UN enter peace negotiations.
14 May	Prime Minister warns that peaceful settlement may not be possible.
17 May	Peace talks continue at UN as Mrs Thatcher speaks of 'one last go'.
19 May	UN peace initiative founders.
20 May	Mrs Thatcher accuses Argentina of 'obduracy and delay, deception and bad faith'. British task force ordered into battle.
21 May	British establish bridgehead at Port San Carlos, E. Falkland.
27 May	Darwin, Goose Green, Douglas and Teal inlet all taken by British.
4 June	Britain vetoes Panamanian-Spanish ceasefire resolution in UN Security Council.
15 June	Argentine garrison at Port Stanley surrenders, bringing cessation of fighting.
20 June	Britain re-takes South Sandwich Island.

The Questionnaire

In June 1937, W.H. Auden, Louis Aragon, Stephen Spender and Nancy Cunard circulated a questionnaire to 150 writers in Britain, asking:

'Are you for, or against, the legal Government and the People of Republican Spain?

'Are you for, or against, Franco and Fascism?'

The answers — mainly for, some against, and a few indifferent to the cause of the Republic — were published in a small book entitled *Authors Take Sides on the Spanish War.*

In 1966 it occurred to Cecil Woolf and John Bagguley that a similar book on the war in Vietnam might prove a useful record of the views of writers — in fact a cross-section of the intellectual community — as well as being a contribution to debate at the time. Observing no censorship, no restriction in style and content of reply, more than 250 authors gave voice to a wide range of thought and feeling: sober reflection, disinterested rejection, satire, sophistry, all possible emotion and none at all.

These two books were of more than passing interest, as may be seen from the enclosed page of excerpts.

Following these precedents we are writing now to about 100 well-known authors in Britain and the United States requesting a brief answer to the questions:

Are you for, or against, our Government's response to the Argentine annexation of the Falkland Islands?

How, in your view, should the dispute in the South Atlantic be resolved?

We intend to publish the replies as a small book to appear in the summer; and would warmly welcome your contribution.

The 1937 Questionnaire

The Questionnaire for *Authors Take Sides on the Spanish War*

THE QUESTION

To the Writers and Poets of England, Scotland, Ireland and Wales

It is clear to many of us throughout the whole world that now, as certainly never before, we are determined or compelled, to take sides. The equivocal attitude, the Ivory Tower, the paradoxical, the ironic detachment, will no longer do.

We have seen murder and destruction by Fascism in Italy, in Germany — the organization there of social injustice and cultural death — and how revived, imperial Rome, abetted by international treachery, has conquered her place in the Abyssinian sun. The dark millions in the colonies are unavenged.

Today, the struggle is in Spain. Tomorrow it may be in other countries — our own. But there are some who, despite the martyrdom of Durango and Guernica, the enduring agony of Madrid, of Bilbao, and Germany's shelling of Almeria, are still in doubt, or who aver that it is possible that Fascism may be what it proclaims it is: 'the saviour of civilization'.

This is the question we are asking you:

Are you for, or against, the legal Government and the People of Republican Spain?

Are you for, or against, Franco and Fascism?

For it is impossible any longer to take no side.

Writers and Poets, we wish to print your answers. We wish the world to know what you, writers and poets, who are amongst the most sensitive instruments of a nation, feel.

Aragon	Nancy Cunard	Pablo Neruda
W.H. Auden	Brian Howard	Ramón Sender
José Bergamin	Heinrich Mann	Stephen Spender
Jean Richard Bloch	Ivor Montagu	Tristan Tzara

Paris, June 1937

Excerpts from *Authors Take Sides on the Spanish War* and *Authors Take Sides on Vietnam*

Of the 149 answers to the 1937 questionnaire, nine of the more interesting ones are given below. Their tone is not altogether representative of that of the book in which they appeared, the book consisting, for the most part, of straightforward expressions of support for the Spanish Republic. These nine replies, together with nine replies from *Authors Take Sides on Vietnam*, were reprinted on a page which accompanied the Falklands questionnaire.

FOR THE GOVERNMENT

Samuel Beckett

¡UPTHEREPUBLIC!

Cyril Connolly

Fascism is the first process by which the cynical few exploit the idealism of the many, by violence and propaganda through the use of a dictator. Its aim is to maintain the status of the rich by using the poor to fight battles. This cannot be done until the whole nation is rendered both warlike and servile. Those who will not make soldiers are not required; those who are not required are eliminated. What we can learn from Spain is the order and extent of that elimination before the stultifying of the human race can proceed. Intellectuals come first, almost before women and children. It is impossible therefore to remain an intellectual and admire Fascism, for that is to admire the intellect's destruction, nor can one remain careless and indifferent. To ignore the present is to condone the future.

Alastair Crowley

Do what thou wilt shall be the whole of the Law.

Franco is a common murderer and pirate: should swing in chains at Execution Dock.

137

Mussolini, the secret assassin, possibly worse.
Hitler may prove a 'prophet'; time will judge.
Love is the law, love under will.

Aldous Huxley

My sympathies are, of course, with the Government side, especially
the Anarchists; for Anarchism seems to me much more likely to lead
to desirable social change than highly centralised, dictatorial Communism. As for 'taking sides'—the choice, it seems to me, is no
longer between two users of violence, two systems of dictatorship.
Violence and dictatorship cannot produce peace and liberty; they
can only produce the results of violence and dictatorship, results
with which history has made us only too sickeningly familiar.

The choice now is between militarism and pacifism. To me, the
necessity of pacifism seems absolutely clear.

Sean O'Casey

I am, of course, for a phalanx unbreakable round those who think
and work for all men, and I am with the determined faces firing at
the steel-clad slug of Fascism from the smoke and flame of the
barricades.

AGAINST THE GOVERNMENT

Arthur Machen

Mr Arthur Machen presents his compliments and begs to inform that
he is, and always has been, entirely for General Franco.

Evelyn Waugh

I know Spain only as a tourist and a reader of the newspapers. I am
no more impressed by the 'legality' of the Valencia Government than
are English Communists by the legality of the Crown, Lords and
Commons. I believe it was a bad Government, rapidly deteriorating.
If I were a Spaniard I should be fighting for General Franco. As an
Englishman I am not in the predicament of choosing between two
evils. I am not a Fascist nor shall I become one unless it were the
only alternative to Marxism. It is mischievous to suggest that such a
choice is imminent.

NEUTRAL

T.S. Eliot

While I am naturally sympathetic, I still feel convinced that it is best that at least a few men of letters should remain isolated; and take no part in these collective activities.

Ezra Pound

Questionnaire an escape mechanism for young fools who are too cowardly to think; too lazy to investigate the nature of money, its mode of issue, the control of such issue by the Banque de France and the stank of England. You are all had. Spain is an emotional luxury to a gang of sap-headed dilettantes.

Excerpts from *Authors Take Sides on Vietnam* (1967)

A. Alverez

Containment of China should begin in the United Nations, from which the USA still debars Peking. These oblique confrontations, savagely involving a third country, are gratuitous, devious, and resolve nothing. The handling is clumsy, the methods brutal, the death-rate unspeakable, the expense disproportionate, and the official figure-head, Ky, ludicrous. I suppose it's good — even essential — for General Motors and the American economy as a whole, but it also alienates everyone, from a significant percentage of the American electorate to the as yet uncommitted nations. As an admirer of America and its realism from way back, I find it odd that a Texan poker-player, as shrewd and apparently uninterested in idealism as the President, should be so reluctant to admit the obvious: that the United States is powerful enough not to lose face by negotiating for peace instead of killing for it.

W.H. Auden

. . . My answer to your question is, I suppose, that I believe a negotiated peace, to which the Vietcong will have to be a party, to be possible, but not yet, and that, therefore, American troops, alas, must stay in Vietnam until it is. But it would be absurd to call this answer *mine*. It simply means that I am an American citizen who reads *The New York Times*.

Kingsley Amis

1. Those who favour American withdrawal from Vietnam must either admire communism, or suppose that it is not imperialistic and aggressive, or both. I can do neither. So I support America's present policy.

2. In a peace dictated by America. It may well be impossible to defeat the communists in the field. Fortunately this is not necessary. They have simply to be convinced that they can never win. They will collapse then.

Simone de Beauvoir

In a word: I am absolutely against the intervention of the United States in Vietnam.

The conflict should be resolved by the evacuation of the American forces. Furthermore, Johnson is in my opinion a war criminal quite as guilty as those who were condemned at Nuremberg.

Jules Feiffer

I'm against it. Isn't everybody?

The solution to the problem is so simple that I'm amazed it hasn't occurred to anyone else.

Lyndon Johnson should go on nationwide TV and say to the American people, 'Ah have goofed', thus ending the only real aggression in Vietnam: our own.

If he brings to his withdrawl speech the same tears and regret he brings to his escalation speeches the American people might very well unite behind him and he probably will not be impeached.

Graham Greene

I am completely against the intervention of the United States in Vietnam. I see no excuse whatever for the presence of foreign troops on the soil of this country. The excuse of containing communism does not appeal to me. If the world has to choose between rule by General Motors or rule by the communist states I prefer to belong to an unaligned country.

In my opinion the conflict in Vietnam can only be resolved by the complete and unconditional withdrawal of American troops. What kind of elections are then held is for the Vietnamese people to decide for themselves. The division between North and South is a very artificial one, but if there are elements in the South which wish to continue a civil war let them do it without Western aid. Such a war would soon come to an end.

Iris Murdoch

The American war in Vietnam is one of the more wantonly wicked political actions of the human race, appalling in its cold-bloodedness and alarming insofar as it is tolerated by a majority of persons in the moderately enlightened democratic country whose instrument of policy it is. From the technical point of view of international justice, since the Americans have no legitimate business in Vietnam and on their own admission prevented the holding of free elections since they objected to the government which the Vietnamese people were likely freely to elect, the war is a war of unjustified aggression on the part of the USA. However, the callous will argue about technicalities. What is important is to stop being callous and keep in mind that on every single day of this vicious war innocent people are being killed and maimed, and that the resources of modern technology are being deployed not to help but to shatter the tenuous civilization of a backward peasant country. Self-interest should check the Americans here. What is a military base compared with the hatred of half a continent? But plain morality also demands an end to a policy which causes such a mountain of suffering. If the American government had any serious will to end this war they could solve the problems involved in ending it. Or are they the slaves of the machine of evil which they have set up?

Harold Pinter

The Americans should not have gone in, but they did.
 They should now get out, but they won't.

Simon Raven

Since England has abdicated from Empire yet failed to align herself with Europe, she has become a client kingdom of America. It is a rash client who opposes the policies of a munificent protector.
 I was once taught, as a young professional soldier, that military failure must never be reinforced. I was also taught that it must never be confessed.

Index